JUST A SHADOW

Amy Curran

First published in 2018 by Pink Coffee Publishing Australia
ISBN-13: 978-0-6482393-8-3
Just A Shadow

© Copyright Amy Curran 2018
The moral right of the Author has been asserted.

All rights reserved. No part of this book may be reproduced or transmitted by any person or entity in any form, by any means, electronic or mechanical, including photocopying, recording, scanning or by any information storage and retrieval system, without prior permission in writing from the publisher.

Cataloguing-in-Publication entrry is available from the
National Library of Australia http://catalogue.nla.gov.au

To Shadow
and all of those without a voice

To my husband Scott
whose crazy idea it was to go and look at a
Stallion because 'it made sense' you changed
my life in so many ways

CHAPTER ONE

I still remember the very first day that I felt the crisp air of this world. It's crazy how things can come full circle. That first day, finding my feet and learning to use my legs... who would have known that 21 years later I would be doing the same.

I was born under the glorious Australian sky. The very first thing I remember was opening my eyes to a bright, wide expanse of blue. I lay on a bed of green, lush grass, as my mother nuzzled her nose against me.

From the moment I found my hooves and started to walk, I loved people.

I remember getting called "pest" a bit, but I just loved seeing what the people got up to. New visitors were especially interesting, we got lots of visitors at the stud where I was born, and I had competition to get their attention!

My master used to laugh at my boldness. Sometimes the visitors were a little nervous, but mostly they laughed too. Mother would let me go and watch as my gangly legs went in all directions when people arrived.

"His name is Shadow", master would say to the visitors. "Because he thinks he is a shadow".

My mother was a beautiful mare. I remember her being a cool grey colour, with small red flecks through her coat. I didn't have the same red flecks she had, I had large red patches. Mother told me that her flecks were once large patches too, but they faded over time until she was mostly that sharp cool grey colour, with small red flecks all over.

"Will my patches fade too mother?" I asked her one day.

"No my darling boy, your patches will gleam bright your whole life." She replied.

My Father was a strong stallion, he was not grey like mother, or patchy like me. He was an iridescent gold colour. He gleamed. He was a well-known horse just like my Grandfather. I had a lot to live up to!

Fathers name was Sandman. He became famous when he was chosen to be the "lotto horse". He was chosen by the Lottery business to be on television in all of their advertisements. They were such proud days for our family.

My Grandfather was known as Rebel, he was also a gleaming gold colour, with the same creamy coloured mane and tail. They were like Palominos, but more gold, richer. The colour was called Flaxen. Everyone wanted a flaxen foal, they were the most popular of all of the colours when I was born. I was a disappointment to my family from that very first day.

As well as being "the wrong colour" I was not the most agile of foals. I struggled to work out how to move my legs in the right way, and constantly ended up either with my nose in the dust or my legs splayed out in all directions.

Mother would softly whinny at me. She was lovely my mother. But Father and Grandfather would snort their disgust.

The man who owned us, we referred to him as Master, knew that my father and grandfather hated me. He would do his best to make sure they were separate from me. But their teasing over the fence still hurt me.

Father would laugh at me when I tried to prance around, Grandfather would be so amused he would stamp his feet in the dust. The dust would come through the fence and make it even harder for me to see where I was going, so I would fall on my face.

One day, while I was practicing my prance, I fell through the fence into Grandfathers paddock. He picked me up with his mouth, grabbed my neck in his teeth and shook me! It hurt so bad. He shook me for a long time, then opened his mouth and I crashed to the hard ground.

My helpless mother stood shocked over the fence line.

Master ran out to see what the noise was, and rescued me from Grandfathers paddock. I had bruises all over and I could barely move from the pain in my back. Every time I tried to stand, it was agony.

The veterinarian was called to see me, and they found I had a very bad spine injury. The vet said I would make a full recovery and it would not affect me later as long as I was made to rest and heal.

Masters wife cared for me for the next few weeks, she would rub my body and I would close my eyes. Her hands were so gentle and her voice as she spoke to me was so soft.

Mother could not stand up to Father and Grandfather. They were both much bigger than her. Mother was helpless. She comforted me as much as she could, whinnying in my ear, telling me that I was strong, and that one day I would be big like them too. Big, strong and admired for who I was.

CHAPTER TWO

My days as a carefree foal seemed to go so fast now that I look back at them. Bounding around in the paddock alongside mother, and playing with the other foals. Visitors most weekends, that was my whole world. It was the only world I knew. I often think about the different paths that my life took me on and how different it may have been had an alternate path been chosen for me. I don't regret my life at all. Everything you go through in life surely shapes you to become the soul you are, but I do wonder if I were meant to endure so much pain in my life to become the horse I am.

My first journey out into the world was about to begin.

Mother explained that most of the visitors who came to our farm where looking to take us home to their farm, to live with them. They would come and see all the foals. Sometimes even a few times, and then decide which one they wanted.

"So they will take you as well?" I naively asked Mother.

"Oh my dear son," she replied, "you won't need me soon. You are going to grow and leave this farm with a new family."

I was shocked! Leave mother? And Master and Masters Wife?

"There's things I still need to teach you my son, and I need you to listen carefully. There are many kinds of people in the big wide world. Some of them good, like Master, who will treat you with respect and care for you. But there are bad ones too, not so nice ones. They will test your patience and your strength, but you must never hurt a person. Even if they hurt you, you must be strong. No good comes to horses who rebel.
I hope with all the hope in the world you find a good person, but I cannot predict this. No matter what though, be yourself, the kind, sweet caring horse you are. Make me proud my son".

I could hear the sadness in her voice, even though she was trying to hide it.

The weeks went on and without realising it straight away, I was relying on mother less and less. I would spend most of the day with the other foals, playing, exploring, and nibbling on the grass. The grass and Master's buckets had soon squashed my desire for mother's milk, and my independence was becoming more evident.

One particular day, Master and his wife came and took mother out of the paddock. As they walked her through the gate way, she turned her head slowly and glanced back at me. I stopped grazing and stared at her. Her eyes were almost bittersweet, a proud moment for her that she had raised me to now be on my own, but encased in a deep sadness, knowing that it may be the last time she would see me.

They came back and took the other mares too. We wondered

where they were going, however we were not sad or stressed about it. Mother had told me that this day would come, she said it was the first step to becoming a strong stallion and making her proud.

Life was fun with my energetic friends, we would spend most of each day just racing each other around the fence line. When I was not in a race, I would be at the far end of the paddock where the driveway forked to the house or the stables. There was a lush apple tree there, it was my best kept secret. None of the other foals had discovered the delicious fruit and I was careful to not let them see me go for a snack.

I assumed the other foals thought it was a tree like any other on our farm. The rest were large Gum trees, with long green leaves. I loved the smell of gum leaves, but they didn't taste anything like a juicy apple.

On the other side of the boundary fences of the farm, all you could see were thick masses of gum trees. I heard Master call it 'the bush' once, it looked so thick that a horse would not be able to move inside. I wondered what animals lived in there, and what was beyond where I could not see.

On weekends, the visitors would come, and the other foals would run around all trying to outdo each other to get the attention of the audience. Not me, I craved cuddles. I would stand at the fence line where the visitors were, while they stroked my face and neck.

"Oh Shadow," Master would say, "you're a soft one aren't you. I hope the world is kind to you."

At the time I didn't understand what he meant, it worried me a little. Why would the world not be kind? Sadly, twenty years later, I do now understand what he meant.

CHAPTER THREE

There was one particular day, I remember two ladies came to look at the fillies. I had overheard them say they were only interested in the girls, but I decided to have some fun. I shadowed them everywhere they went. Every filly they looked at.

"Lisa he wants to come home with you!" one of the ladies said.

The lady who was called Lisa laughed, and turned to give me a big pat. She turned so fast it surprised me and I jumped sideways, nearly falling over. They both laughed.

"You are a beautiful boy, with such striking markings! I'm sorry buddy I can't take you now, I just don't have the spare money, maybe we will see each other again some day." Lisa said. I hoped so, she was fun. As they left the paddock and walked towards their car, I neighed as loud as I could. They both turned and giggled.

A new daily routine presented, and the other foals and I started on our education. We learnt to wear a halter, an interesting webbing of material that went behind our ears and around our noses. It was very strange, it made my nose feel heavy. I wasn't the most balanced of foals, Masters Wife used to say I was 'clumsy' and she would laugh. With a heavy halter on my nose I was even funnier it seemed. Some of the other foals went a bit crazy they didn't like the halter at all, but Master would come into the paddock with some tasty warm mash in a bucket and they would settle and forget about the halter. If anyone wants to start a foal well, that is how. Master was always so kind and gentle.

At the end of the first week, Master called us all into the sand arena. We trotted through, eager to see as we had only seen it from the outside. One by one he hooked a rope onto each of our halters and tied the other end to rings around the arena. When he tied my rope on, I turned to follow him, but the rope pulled me tight. I was stuck! I looked at the rope in horror, I pulled again, but I couldn't move away!

Masters Wife came to me and slowly rubbed my neck, "There there Shadow, it's ok. You need to learn this to find your new people. It's very important". I hoped my people would be just like her. Her touch was so comforting, and her voice could almost put me to sleep.

My instinct told me to fight the rope, to pull against the restraint, but I heard mothers voice inside my head "You must be strong, no good comes to horses who rebel" and I relaxed against the rope.

We went through this lesson every day for the next few weeks. Soon we were all experts. Even the foals that were the most head strong, had accepted being tied up, knowing that they weren't stuck there forever.

Early one morning, Master and his wife came to the yards and clicked leads on myself and another colt, Jay. Masters wife rubbed my neck and told me that we were going on a little outing.

"See a bit of the outside world for the day," she said to me.

I was intrigued! Master and his wife led us around to the drive, where the truck and opened trailer were waiting.

"Take him up first," Master said to his wife "he'll follow you anywhere, reckon he'll just go straight on and this one will follow."

That I did. One foot on the ramp... it did feel a little bouncy, I was a little unsure, but Master's wife clicked me up and encouraged me to step again with some fresh green lucerne hay. Up I went the rest of the way and she tied my lead to the link at the front of the trailer. Master came up behind and did up the steel gate at my rump.

Jay was an unusual looking colt. He was a tobiano pattern like me, but his patches were a dark cream Buckskin colour. Buckskins were not commonly seen at this time, so a Buckskin tobiano was an unusual sight. He was slightly smaller than me, as he was two months younger.

"Come on Jay" Masters wife called from inside the float, and Master led him up beside. He walked straight on, up beside me, and Master passed the lead for his wife to tie up at the front. The second steel gate was fixed, and the ramp lifted. Masters wife rubbed both our heads and exited through the side door, closing it gently behind her.

With each other as assurance and company, Jay and I travelled fine and soon arrived at the grounds. The atmosphere was electric at the show and both of us stood wide eyed in the float as the tail gate was lowered. We could hear the show rides, and the bustle and chatter of people off in the distance. The smells... so many smells.

I had heard about show grounds before, overhearing conversations between my Father and Grandfather. They never told me about them, probably because they thought I was not good enough to ever go to a show, but I heard stories when they returned to the farm some weekends.

Master left us in the float with the steel gates behind us, so we were safe and not exposed to it all straight away. We soon settled and became used to the noises and we both enjoyed a nibble at our hay bags.

Masters wife gave us both a nice brushing, including our manes and our fluffy foal tails. She got us out of the trailer one at a time and changed our halters for thin leather show ones. When Master came around the side of the float, he was dressed quite smartly in beige jeans and a shirt. He took my lead and led me out into the ring.

I walked right out to the middle, where a man in a large hat was pointing. Master walked along beside me and together we went in and around in a circle. Once around, then Master led me to the middle in front of a woman who was standing waiting.

Master rubbed my neck, "Good boy Shadow, stand nice and still now."

My ears twitched back and forth from Master, to the lady who was walking slowly around me.

What was she looking at? She sure was interested in what I looked like.

"Thank you, out and back please." The lady said to Master. He pulled my lead and ran out in a straight line. I followed beside him trotting along swishing my tail. At the end of the line we turned, I stumbled a little, but found my feet and headed back to the lady. Master pulled again, gesturing me to stop beside him and the lady nodded, smiling.

I got to go and line up while some other horses stood in front of the lady and then went out and back. When they had finished, they each came and lined up beside me. When the last horse finished and was making its way to our line, the lady went to the man in the large hat and he gave her a bunch of colored straps. They looked like rug straps, but were shinier and didn't look as thick. They had tassel bits on the end of them, so pretty.

The lady came over and put a blue one around my neck.

"Well done Shadow" Master said. "A blue ribbon from the Judge means you got first place."

Ribbon? Oh the strap thing. Judge? I presumed that was the lady.

It seemed like a lot of effort for a quick run around the ring. It was over before we knew it. I had to do this routine in the ring one more time, which was the same as before, except this time I got a bigger ribbon. It had three colors all joined together. Red, white and blue.

I enjoyed the day, but still thought it was a lot of fuss. Masters wife thought I was so clever, and kept shaking the ribbons I had gotten from the Judge around my face, laughing while she hugged me. Jay got ribbons that day too, I think he got a red one. Still, a lot of effort for a flappy thing it seemed!

That night at home, Masters Wife fixed us both an extra scoop of grains, and snuck us both a piece of bread.

CHAPTER FOUR

The first of my paddock mates to leave the farm was a big strong bay colt. I hadn't spent a lot of time with him as he was one of the herd leaders from the very start. I tried to avoid confrontations where I could and mostly hung out with the fillies. I found them easier, I didn't have to prove my strength to them, they were just happy to be my friend.

The afternoon that he left, Master told us that he had gone to a new home, to start his brand new life full of adventures. He said that we would go soon as well, and have a new Master to teach us things and care for us.

Over time my friends left for their new homes, one by one. I wondered why I had not been chosen yet and why I was one of the last to leave the farm. Maybe my Father and Grandfather were right, I was not as good as them.

There were only a few of us left on the day by new master arrived to meet me. His name was Sarge.

Sarge was a strange kind of man, he looked like a man straight out of the bush, kind of what you would imagine Ned Kelly to look like if he were right in front of you. He was tall, a wiry sort of build, with a bushy beard and eyebrows. I stared at him as he walked from his truck to the stables.

"Oo-roo!" I heard him call... "Oo-roo, Les, ya here?"

I heard the fillies behind me giggle. He did sound different to most that had been to visit, he certainly was straight out of the bush!

Master came out and greeted Sarge. They chatted briefly before Master went and fetched a lead and halter for me. I was still staring at Sarge when they came to the paddock gate.

"Come on Shadow, come and say hello," Master called to me. I wandered over, snorting quietly as I went. Eager to see what smells Sarge had brought with him, that may give some clues about where he was from. Especially if it was possibly to be my new home with him. He smelt like smoke. Not fire smoke, the type of smoke that some people had on their clothes. This smoke smell was like that, but a bit stronger. As I got closer to him, I nuzzled his shirt, and my nose bumped his top pocket. A funny shaped object was sticking out the top of it.

Sarge let out a harsh laugh, and Master said, "He wants to try your pipe Sarge!" And laughed along with him.

I had no idea what a pipe was, but it stunk!

Master proceeded to put the halter and lead on me and Sarge went to drop the tailgate on the trailer.

This was not the person I had imagined would be taking me

from the farm, especially after I had done well at the shows. Why was I going with this man? Again, thoughts of my Fathers disappointment clouded my mind, and I accepted my fate. If this was my first experience at a new home, I would make the most of it and do my best.

I walked around to the end of the tailgate and peered inside. There were leaves and twigs all through the inside of the trailer, my suspicions about going bush were pretty spot on I thought. Going bush with the bushie! Haha! What an adventure I was about to start, with my new mate Sarge.

How naïve I was.

CHAPTER FIVE

It didn't seem like we had traveled far, when we arrived at my new home with Sarge. We veered off the main road and bumped along a rocky track, through the bush. Low branches hit the trailer and leaves dropped through the windows on each side. I tried to look through, but every time I did I got whacked with leaves and small twigs. Patiently I looked straight ahead, trying to see through the front window instead. It was clouded up with dust and dirt though, all I could see through the haze was more dust billowing up from the rear tyres of Sarges truck. The dust was a rich red colour, which turned a bright yellow as it rose up and caught the sunlight.

A few minutes later we came to a stop and the dust billowed upwards. I closed my eyes and tried to squeeze my nostrils shut. I heard the truck door close, footsteps, and then the tailgate of the trailer being lowered and hitting the ground.

"C'morn mate," Sarge said "Out ya come and check out ya new place."

He walked up and undid the lead, and I walked backwards out of the trailer, into the dappled light of the bush. Wow.

Just A Shadow

It was beautiful! Our own hideaway. All I could see were large gumtrees, with huge trunks that seemed to go upwards for miles. Sarge led me over to a yard, took off my lead, and left me to explore my new surrounds.

My yard was one of the few cleared areas, everywhere else I could see was covered with gumtrees. There wasn't a lot of grass, and it was a different type of grass to where I grew up. Rocks and fallen branches scattered the ground, and over near the far fence I could see a bathtub, which I assumed was my water. I felt like Denny, the horse from the Man from the Snowy River! With my own man Sarge.

Crunch, snap, crunch

I spun around to see where the noise was coming from, it sounded like crunching leaves and twigs snapping. Out from the trees came a horse, and another, and soon all along the bottom fence line were faces staring at me, wide eyed.

"What sort of horse is he" I heard one mutter.

"Not sure, what colour is he?

"He is like two different colours? Like a patchwork quilt" the first one replied.

I wandered over and introduced myself. It was very clear they had never seen a horse coloured like me. A patchwork quilt though? Haha, I hadn't heard that one before.

The herd consisted of a couple of older geldings, some younger ones and four mares. They were all either brown, bay or chestnut. No patches. Quite a plain looking lot to be honest, but they would become my new family and my first company out in the big world.

There were no other Colts or Stallions at Sarges place, I was it. I could have let that go to my head being the top man around the place, but I was determined not to be like my Father and Grandfather. I treated all my friends with respect and tried to do whatever Sarge asked of me.

Life with Sarge was pretty relaxed, we didn't go anywhere, just stayed around the bush. He seemed to like spending time with me though, sitting outside the yard on a stump, watching me while smoking on his pipe. We didn't get a lot of visitors either, Sarge seemed to like the quiet and didn't often go anywhere. I got used to the twigs and obstacles around my paddock and as the weeks went on I stopped tripping and stumbling so much.

Months went by, and Sarge and I had formed a nice friendship. The unspoken kind of friendship. I respected him, and he respected me, no need for either of us to prove ourselves in any way. Just mates.

CHAPTER SIX

It had been almost a year since I arrived to live with Sarge. I had grown almost a hand and was starting to look more like a young stallion rather than a gangly adolescent colt. Sarge started to work with me in the round yard. The first lessons were so boring. All he would do was lead me around and around and around. I already knew how to walk on a lead, I don't know why he was wasting so much time with it. When I got bored I would get a bit cheeky and when he was in front of me, I would grab the back of his shirt with my teeth. He didn't get mad at me, just laughed. When I realised it made him laugh, I did it all the time.

I was too young to start being ridden yet, so Sarge taught me tricks instead. The first one was so easy. All I had to do was follow him. It was easy. I could follow him with my eyes shut. All I had to do was use my nose and smell that pipe smoke and I knew exactly where he was without even looking. I would follow Sarge around the yard and when he stopped, I stopped. The quicker Sarge stopped, the quicker I stopped. I got to the stage where I would watch his body, waiting for the slightest indication and then stop as quick as I could! I started to stop so fast that sometimes my back legs didn't keep up and kept going! Causing my front legs to jump forward after I had stopped!

This gave Sarge an idea, and he started to teach me to lift my front legs on command, both at the same time. It was hard at first, I was growing into a big horse, and standing just on my back legs took a lot of muscle that I hadn't developed yet.

I really enjoyed standing up, I felt so big and powerful. Sarge had not taught any of the other horses to rear, it was our special trick. Sarge would do a 'clap' with his hands and up I would go! As my muscles grew, I was able to go higher and higher. I was on top of the world. I was keen to rear at any time, just waiting for that clap signal.

Sarge also taught me to 'shake'. He would stand in front of me and touch the front of my leg with his tapping stick while saying 'shake'. When I lifted my hoof, he would praise me.

The seasons went by in the bush, winter brought a cold frost to our home and most of the animals that shared our space went into hiding to escape the chill. The kookaburras were silent, lizards and snakes were nowhere to be seen and the kangaroos only showed themselves after the sun had melted the ice from the ground.

Sarge spent more time indoors, only coming out to check on us in the middle of the day, and throw out some feed. The top of my water would freeze overnight, but I soon learnt to whack it with my hoof, to crack it. The cracked piece would break and sink to the bottom of the old bath tub, leaving a gap just big enough for me to drink through.

Thankfully the cold didn't last long, and I got to see Sarge more often again. In the mornings, as the sun first came through I would wake to the sound of his kettle whistling, and soon after he would come outside.

We had a new routine now, instead of tricks, Sarge was teaching me how to carry things on my back. Every morning I would walk into the yard and Sarge would put different objects on top of my back, towels, heavy sacks, and watch how I would react. I wasn't worried about them at all, so Sarge started rubbing them all over. Up and down my legs, around my shoulders, and around my tail.

I got used to the rubs and soft blankets, so the first time Sarge put a leather saddle on me I got a bit of a shock! It was hard! Hard, heavy, and cold. It had metal stirrups on it that clanged as I moved. I didn't like it at all. But, I put up with it for my mate Sarge.

The morning that he did up the girth for the first time though, no, I couldn't put up with that! He buckled it up and unclipped my lead, clicking me off into a trot around the yard. It was horrible! It bounced as I cantered, the metal stirrups hitting my sides. I gave a buck, and another, trying to get it off me, but it didn't budge.

Every day I had to go through the same process, and every day I tried to get it off. I hated the girth especially, it was done up so tight that I felt I could hardly breathe. Sarge persevered for weeks, the same routine every day and eventually I give up trying to get it off. My back was sore, and I had rubs from the girth. My sides were bruised from the stirrups clanging around.

The day I stopped fighting it, Sarge rewarded me with a warm mash of grains and bran. Maybe it wasn't so bad after all. I could try and get used to it.

I learnt that it was much easier to accept the saddle and not buck and carry on. If I just walked around the yard, the stirrups wouldn't move nearly as much, and would barely hurt my sides at all. If I didn't buck, the saddle wouldn't bounce as much, and it wouldn't hit my back so hard when it came back down. And then, at the end of the morning, I would get a nice bucket of mash.

The first time that Sarge climbed up on to my back I got very nervous. I had seen him on top of the other horses, but I did not think that he would be climbing on me. I was not at all sure how I felt about it, but wanted to try and do my best.

So, I did as I was taught, and stood up! I performed a beautiful rear, just as Sarge had taught me, he was sure to be impressed I thought.

THUD

Oh no! Sarge fell off my back! He hit the ground hard, and groaned. Had I hurt him? Did I do something wrong?

Sarge eventually got up, and was not happy. He grabbed my bridle and lead me over to the fence, not saying a word. He took off the saddle and left me in the yard. Where was my mash? There was no mash. I did not understand at all.

He left me in the yard a good few days, maybe three or four, I can't quite remember. I was miserable. The other horses stared at me, they didn't understand either. I could hear Sarge inside the house, but he didn't come out as much as usual. I was so hungry, what had I done wrong?

Eventually Sarge came out into the yard and gave me a pat on the neck. It was comforting, and I was happy that he was there with me, but he wasn't the same. He moved around to the rail of the yard and pulled off the saddle. He hesitantly put it on my back and clinched up the girth. Then, he stood back a while and huffed on his pipe, watching me. I watched him back.

Was this a new game? He looked rather serious. Moments passed, Sarge blinked, I blinked. I desperately wanted to make him happy again.

Soon enough, he came over and put the bridle on over my halter. He led me around a few times and then out into the middle of the yard. We stopped, and he ran his hand up over my face, putting the reins over and down my neck, to the front of the saddle. I heard him breathe a sigh of relief. I didn't know what for.

Then, he quickly put his foot in the stirrup and jumped himself up into the saddle, quickly finding the stirrup with his other foot. He seemed very rigid as he gave me a squeeze with his calves and off we went into a brisk walk.

Sarge had not ridden me out of the yard yet and I could tell that day wasn't going to be today. I hoped it was soon though, I desperately wanted to explore the tracks around the bush.

Before I knew it, we were done. Sarge dismounted in the middle of the yard and led me back to the rail. Bored, but satisfied I didn't disappoint him, I stood while he removed the saddle, cloth and bridle. He walked out of the yard, and a few moments later returned with mash! Happiness is a bucket of mash.

The next few times Sarge came to ride me, went about the same. Just a few laps of walk and done. However, one windy morning, he attached some extra reins to my bit. The extra reins ran straight across to the girth of the saddle and were fixed tight. I couldn't lift my head! They were very uncomfortable, and I was concerned what the point of them was. Up he went, climbing into the saddle and squeezed me up into a walk.

I was so confused! Sarge was squeezing me with the command to walk forward, yet the horrible side reins were telling me to stop! I chomped on the bit, hoping Sarge would see that I was stressed and take them off. His squeezes turned into kicks and he forcefully pushed me into a brisk walk. I pulled against the reins, but it was hopeless, I could barely see where I was going, and my eyes were hurting from the strain of trying to look up.

I was breathing heavy now, as he pushed me hard into a trot. I jig jogged around the yard, I couldn't stride out at all with the reins attached, I felt so restricted. As we went around, the wind knocked a branch down onto one of the gates, I jumped in fright! The reins pulled my head hard and I lost my balance, falling right over backwards. Sarge fell out of the saddle and hit the ground, I couldn't see where he was, it all happened so quickly, and the reins were holding my head tight. I landed on top of Sarge.

The next few hours went so slowly, I was stuck on the ground, my head held in position by the reins still attached and I could not get my balance to get up. Sarge pulled himself up, he was making the most painful noises, I had really hurt him, and I couldn't say sorry. He must have made it back into the house, as soon after an Ambulance arrived, siren sounding loudly, and took him away.

I laid there in the yard, sad, worried and unable to move. My stomach panged with hunger pains and my throat was dry, I was so thirsty.

As the light was fading a car came up the drive, and a man got out and came to me. I had seen him only a few times, a friend of Sarges that only visited occasionally, although compared to how many visitors he had overall he would have been the most frequent. He entered the yard and undid the side reins. I jumped up and shook. I could feel every muscle release, and the blood rushing through my legs. The man unsaddled me and put me back in my paddock.

I went to the bathtub for a huge drink.

CHAPTER SEVEN

After this, Sarge decided to find me a new home. He said that I was too much for him, he had broken some of his ribs the day he fell and the ambulance came. I had tried so hard to do what he wanted, I guess I just didn't understand.

I felt so bad that I hurt Sarge and even worse that I would not get the chance now to make it up to him. He stopped coming to my paddock to feed me and would only check my water with a passing glance

I felt hungry all the time. There was minimal grass in my paddock, just red dirt and broken twigs and branches.

A lot of people came to look at me over the next few weeks, no one rode me though. I heard one woman whisper "You heard he is the dangerous horse, I really don't think we should".

Dangerous? I could not believe my ears. They must have thought I hurt Sarge on purpose. I was devastated. I would never hurt Sarge, or anyone else, on purpose.

Lots of other visitors talked about my nice colour and markings, but then they would discuss how skinny I was. No one took me with them. I was feeling sad, I longed to prove to a new home that I was a good boy, not a dangerous horse like others had said.

My chance came the day that Betty came to see me. She caught my eye as soon as she got out of her truck, long blonde hair, like a flaxen horse. A man was with her, who I would come to know as Craig.

Betty was talking to Sarge as they walked towards my paddock and I overheard her tell him that her friend had been a few days before. Bettys friend had told her that she had to come and look at me, as she thought I would make her a nice foal with her horse, but she couldn't have a stallion full time. Craig unlatched the gate and held it open for Betty. She walked through and straight towards me. She obviously didn't think I was a dangerous horse! Craig asked Sarge to saddle me up, and put me through my paces. As he went to get the gear, Betty stroked my neck and looked straight into my eyes.

"Hey beautiful boy, you don't seem so bad" she whispered, almost putting me to sleep with her soothing voice. I pushed her gently with my head and she laughed.

Sarge returned carrying the saddle, bridle and cloth and placed them on the rail of the yard. He came over and gave Betty the halter and lead, and she placed it over my head, and lead me into the yard.

Sarge hadn't really touched me since his accident and seemed very nervous. I think Betty and Craig picked up on it too, as they were watching him quite intently. He fumbled around with the bridle, pushed the bit into my mouth, lifted the straps over my head and buckled up the throat latch. I tried to stand patiently, but I could feel how nervous Sarge was and his tension was feeding into me.

"I ahh, I wont put his saddle on, I'll just quickly show ya his moves eh?" Sarge said to Betty and Craig.

They nodded.

He pulled me over to the stump in the middle of the yard, clambered up onto it, then onto my back. I think Sarge ditched the saddle so he could jump off me in a hurry if he needed to, he really didn't seem happy about being up on my back. It must have been uncomfortable up there too, my backbone protruding the way it was from my loss of weight. We walked around a few times, both directions, and did a few paces of trot each way. By a few paces, I mean around ten steps in total. Sarge couldn't get off me quick enough.

He steered me back to where Betty and Craig were standing and slid down. He handed my reins to Craig and said "I'll ah, leave you two to make a decision eh?" And scuttled off to fetch his pipe from the verandah.

Betty and Craig looked at each other with raised eyebrows.

"Well, that was something else" said Betty.

"Yeah you could say that!" Craig replied. "I wonder why he was so nervous? He really didn't want to be up there did he?"

Just A Shadow

"No I don't think so," Betty sounded concerned. "I don't know what the story is, but we can't leave this poor boy here, he is lovely look at him. We have to give him a future, and a good feed!"

And with that, I had found my new home.

CHAPTER EIGHT

Craig and Betty came back the following day with their trailer. I was so excited! I couldn't wait to see what their place was like. I bet there were other horses. I watched as Craig exchanged paperwork and money with Sarge and Betty prepared the trailer, putting down the tail gate, and moving the divider across. It was a very clean trailer inside, it looked very comfortable.

Sarge and Craig finished their business and Betty came into the paddock to put a halter and lead on me. Craig got the gate and she led me through over to the float. I couldn't wait to get inside!

"Hey!" Betty said to me sharply. "Where are your manners!"

I halted abruptly at the firmness of her voice.

"You wait please, take your time, one step at a time, none of this bull at a gate caper thank you."

Sarge looked impressed, Craig was smiling. I loved her.

We didn't seem to be on the road for long, when we slowed into a tree lined driveway. I peered through the window and could still see bushland, but it was a different type of bush. Big tall trees, but no scrub. Instead, in between the trees were large green paddocks, of thick lush grass.

The truck and trailer came to a stop in front of a cream coloured shed and I listened as the truck doors opened and closed.

"Welcome to Pleasant Valley" Betty said to me as she came through the door at the front of the trailer. I heard Craig lower the tailgate and Betty came and undid my lead from the tie. I waited for her instruction and stepped back slowly, finding my footing as I went. It was afternoon and as I walked backwards and came out of the trailer I could see the suns rays streaming through the trees. I saw mares in the green paddocks and a couple of foals bounded around, hardly noticing my arrival.

Betty led me down the drive and into a small yard behind the shed. She unclicked my lead and rubbed my neck.

"Settle in now boy, I'll be back to check on you later."

The sun slowly set the whole way down, and the warm night brought with it a calm around my new home. The only sounds were soft grazing and the occasional frog. I closed my eyes, feeling comfort and fell into a deep sleep.

As the sun rose from the horizon, the parrots started their morning chatter and woke me from my sleep. Wow it was a good sleep! I looked out across the paddocks I could see and admired what was before me.

Betty came around the corner with a big bucket of feed.

I gave a low whinny, expressing my appreciation. I hadn't had a bucket of feed for a while, not since before Sarges accident. I hadn't had much at all, just the bush grasses that were scattered throughout my paddock. She leaned over the rails and poured the feed into a hanging feeder. I pushed my head into the gourmet mix.... corn, grains, seeds, chaff, and... was that molasses? I was in heaven! I got through the feed quickly, there wasn't much in there.

Betty returned to check my water and laughed when she saw my empty feeder and the molasses still around my nose, "Oh you liked that did you?! You can have some more tonight, only small feeds to start, don't want you getting a belly ache."

She finished topping up my water and left me to enjoy the sun on my back. The full sun was glorious, I had only felt dappled light in the bush, the full sun was so warm.

Later in the day Craig came and took me out to one of the paddocks. He unclicked my lead and let me go for a run alone. The grass was like a giant sponge, so soft! I lifted my legs high, prancing through the sea of green. The mares were watching, I snorted as I trotted past them, tail high, and neck arched proud. I did a full lap and came to a walk. The smell of the rich grass was too tempting, and I stuck my head down for a feed.

When Betty came to get me from the paddock, I wasn't feeling so good. I groaned as she clicked on the lead to the halter, and she looked at me worried.

"Are you ok Shadow? Is something wrong" she asked.

I turned my head and hit the side of my stomach with my nose.

"Oh dear, a belly ache, you've eaten too much haven't you" Betty said. She led me to the yard and unclicked me while she went to fetch a rug for me to wear overnight.

Ouch! A spasm in my stomach hit me. It was so painful I wanted to curl up in a ball. I dropped to the ground, rolling, trying to make the pain stop.

Betty heard me fall and ran to the yard. "Craig! Craig! I need you!" She screamed.

As she clicked the lead back on, Craig rounded the corner and entered the yard. Together they encouraged me up, made me get back on my feet. The pain was too much, I just wanted to stay on the ground.

"He is collicking Craig, quick call the vet!" Betty cried. Craig raced to the house to use the phone. As he ran, Betty pulled hard on my lead.

"Stay up Shadow, come on! You have to stay up!" I tried to do as Betty said but I was in agony. I just wanted to roll and release the pain.

Craig came back out of the house and said the vet was on the way. I pawed the ground with my hoof, trying to release my pain that way.

After what seemed an eternity, a big white fourwheel drive came hurtling up the drive way. A man in blue overalls got out and came over to me carrying a large bag. He checked my temperature and looked me all over, then said that he would administer a pain injection.

Injection? I didn't like the sound of that!

Before I realised what was happening, I felt a sharp jab! The man had stabbed me with a needle! I wanted to react, but then I felt the pain easing, not completely but it was definitely easing. I still had the desire to roll, but I think I could bare to stand a little longer. I closed my eyes.

Blergh! I was awoken to a disgusting taste in my mouth! The man in the overalls had squirted something horrible in while my eyes were closed! I was too weak to resist though, so I just screwed my nose up in disgust.

"Don't let him go down Betty, keep him up." He said to Betty. "You'll know when it has passed, just keep on him, don't give up on him. Call again if you need me."

And he left.

The day turned into night, Betty was by my side the whole time.

Craig came out in the middle of the night, took my lead and told her to get some rest. He took over for a while, walking, and walking some more. Up and down the driveway, around the lanes between the paddocks, and around the sheds. I was exhausted.

Occasionally I tried to lay down, but Craig was on to me.

"No mate, come on, its for the best, you gotta stay up."

I trusted Craig and Betty, even though I had just arrived, I knew in my heart they were good people as soon as I saw them.

Daylight started to stream through the trees and Betty raced from the house.

"How is he?" She asked Craig, panting.

"Still upright!" Craig replied, "exhausted, and still seems to be in a fair amount of pain, but he is upright."

"Ill take over now, you go inside" and Betty took the lead.

The pain continued, day turned into night again, and then into day. When was it going to stop? I didn't want to die when I had just arrived in such a glorious place. Pleasant Valley was beautiful, the lush grass, the trees and sun rays...

Humph!

I fell to the ground.

"Shadow no! Shadow get up!" Betty cried.

I could not, this was the end I knew it. Why. Why was I in so much pain, it wasn't going to stop, I started to close my eyes.

"NO! I will not let you die on me! Get up NOW!" She pulled on my lead as hard as she could, I opened my eyes slightly and could see her crying.

The last thing I wanted to do was make her cry. I lifted my head and pulled my front legs up in front of my chest. With an excruciating move, I heaved myself up off the ground.

Betty laughed amongst her tears, "Yes! Good boy! Come on!"

I had to pull through the pain for her, I think she really loved me already.

The pain lasted for four whole days. Craig and Betty took turns walking me, making sure I stayed upright and moving. I'd never felt such a constant pain for so long, a pain that numbed my entire body. The exhaustion from walking constantly was enough by itself, without the added internal pain. Inside and out, I was numbed.

Craig called the vet to come and give me another look over, make sure it had passed. The man arrived and after putting the stethoscope to my stomach, gave me the all clear.

"Let him rest now, but keep an eye on him for any signs ok." Betty nodded, and the vet left.

Betty turned to Craig. "I blame myself, I should have realised he was not used to such rich feed."

"Oh, sweetheart you weren't to know, how could we know he wasn't fed before he came here." Craig said to Betty.

"It was obvious! You saw his paddock and that silly man! I only gave him a small feed, but then with the lush grass on top, it was too much. He wouldn't have had grass like that for a while!" Betty cried.

It wasn't Bettys fault at all, I walked over to her and pushed her with my head. She ran her hand along my cheek.

"See, he doesn't blame you." Craig smiled.

CHAPTER NINE

The proceeding weeks were uneventful compared to those first few days. Craig and Betty allowed me to settle in and get used to my new home. Once I had become used to the pasture, they allowed me to spend days and nights out in the paddock. King of my own domain, it felt good.

Craig started to do some handling work with me, mainly just walking around, teaching me to walk alongside him. He told me that I had to learn some manners. I remember Betty had asked me where my manners were the day she picked me up from Sarges. I wasn't sure, I didn't know where I could have gotten 'manners' from or what they were. Maybe they were like shoes? The farrier came and put those on the riding horses, was there a 'manners man' that delivered manners?

"We may need some extra help with him Betty," I heard Craig say one afternoon. "He is a sweet horse, but he really needs some boundaries. What the man taught him was no good for a Stallion, far too dangerous."

There was that dangerous word again. I was not dangerous!

Betty agreed and said she would call their trainer friend Josh, to see if he could help.

A few days later Josh arrived. I watched as he got out of his truck, and noticed he had someone with him on the other side. A little dog ran out from around the car, what a funny looking thing! A lady followed calling the dog, I recognised her voice. I craned my neck to see, it was Lisa! The lady I followed that day when I was a foal! I called out to her!

"He hasn't changed one bit!" Lisa laughed to Betty as she walked towards me. "Hey fella, good to see you again. Haven't you turned into a fine specimen. How old is he now, would he be six?"

"Yes that's right, six now, we adore him." Betty replied.

"How are you going with him" Lisa asked.

"Ok, he has a beautiful nature, such a friendly boy, just has no manners at all." Betty said.

"A friend I know looked at him, but that would not have been a good match. He taught him to rear did he not?"

"Rear? Oh I didn't hear about that." Betty said.

"Oh brother, and shake hands too I heard, recipe for disaster, especially with a Stallion. How is the man after the accident, he ok?" Lisa asked.

"Accident?" Replied Betty, confused.

"You didn't know?" Lisa said. "He fell off Shadow after he

reared in the yard. Silly sod of a man. Serves him right for teaching him such a silly trick. Poor horse got a fast reputation of being dangerous, should have been the man that got a reputation for being a silly sod! Shadow was only doing as he was taught."

I liked Lisa, she kept tabs on me, how special. I was glad she was here. Poor Betty though hadn't heard about why Sarge sold me. She was upset that he did not tell her the truth.

"Well he is here now!" Betty laughed. "Think we can make a respectable horse out of him?"

Lisa nodded and they walked over to Josh and Craig, who were chatting near the shed.

"Righto, lets get to work" Josh said to Lisa, and they walked to the truck to get some gear. I watched as they walked to the round yard with a bunch of ropes, varying lengths, a whip, and a couple of different halters.

Betty came and got me from the paddock, and lead me into the yard, where she handed my lead to John, and then went outside the yard, closing the gate. She joined Lisa and Craig on the other side.

I wasn't afraid of Josh, he seemed a sensible man. I decided to show him what I already knew, so he didn't have to teach me those things. I pawed the ground...

"Stop!" Said Josh sharply.

Hang on, hang on, I thought. I am not done, I'm trying to show you something. I pawed the ground again, and lifted my leg high.

"I said STOP" said Josh, and he tapped me on my knee with the whip.

Hey! Why did he do that for?

"You must learn to do as your handler says Shadow, I know you know some party tricks, but party tricks will not make you a good horse. You need to respect your master above all else." Josh said to me.

I listened intently. He moved to my shoulder and and said "walk", as he pulled my lead. But I didn't want to walk, I wanted to show him what else I could do.

"Walk!" Josh said firmly and tapped my side with the whip. I jumped forward. "Good!" He praised. "Good boy Shadow! Good listening."

He just wanted me to literally walk? How demeaning! Did he think I knew nothing? Every horse knows how to walk, I know tricks! I am special!

As we moved around the yard, I tried again. I propped my front legs, up, up....

"NO!" Josh said firmly again.

Argh, righto, I give up for now. Have it your way, lets do your boring walk, I thought to myself. We walked a few boring laps, and Josh stopped and gave me a pat.

"Good boy, well done." He said.

Really? That's it? I wondered. I think that was it. Josh handed me back to Betty who came into the yard with a brush.

"Lots of that to start" Josh said. "Back to basics for him, consistency will be the key, then we will start desensitising him to the trick commands."

He walked out of the yard and towards Lisa.

"Bye Shadow! See ya again tomorrow Betty," Lisa yelled as she walked with Josh to their truck.

Betty tied me to the rail and brushed me all over. It felt good. Although I was not tired, we didn't actually do anything physical, I think my brain was tired. It was confusing trying to understand what Josh wanted and didn't want, me to do. Did he really only want me to walk quietly beside him? That seemed way too simple.

Josh returned every day for the next couple of weeks, but after the first few days he included Craig and Betty in my training as well. I was getting the hang of the exercises and was learning that the tricks I knew... was what they didn't want me to do. I think the tricks were bad. People shook hands though, why didn't they want me to shake hands?

At the end of the second week, Josh said that he didn't need to come every day now, and for Craig and Betty to call when they wanted him. I had grown to like Josh, he was a simple man. No fuss and very calm.

I did enjoy having Craig and Betty all to myself again too though.

CHAPTER TEN

Spring was a glorious time at Pleasant Valley. The farm was bustling with birds, butterflies and wild rabbits that hip hopped through the paddocks. Last seasons foals had been weaned from their mothers and were enjoying chasing the rabbits through the long grass. I contently watched the happenings of the farm, not a care in the world, life was good.

One morning I awoke to the sound of a large horse truck coming up the driveway. It was one of those big semi trailers that went interstate, long distances, brought horses from far away. I watched as the driver got out and Craig went down to greet him. They chatted a while, and then moved to open one of the side doors of the truck. The driver went inside.

Soon he came back out leading a very large mare. She was dark brown in colour and had thick strong legs with white stockings. Around her legs were white feathering, longer hairs that shaped her legs down to her hooves. Her hooves echoed as she slowly made her way down the ramp.

I called out loudly, trying to get her attention and let her know I was here. She turned and looked at me, unfazed, she was so calm. Her neck was so big too! And her mane and tail were as black as the wheels on the truck she had came out of.

Betty must have heard my welcome neigh and she came running from the house. "She is here!"

The driver handed the lead to Betty. "She is, and you'll be pleased to know she travelled well."

"Thank you" Betty replied, "I appreciate your care, she is big isn't she! Hope Shadow can reach her!" They all laughed.

I wasn't sure what she meant by that, I just wanted to say hello close up. I called out again, louder this time, and shook my mane. That got her attention, and she pricked her ears towards me. Betty led her over to my fence line to say hello, and I showed my appreciation with a snort and another shake of my mane.

"You like her Shadow? This is Tara. She is a big girl isn't she." Betty said.

I sniffed down her neck, and raised my top lip to smell the air around her. She was simply majestic.

"I'm going to put her in the yard for now Shadow, you'll get to meet her closer in a few days, that will be interesting." Betty giggled as she led her away.

I watched Tara from a distance for the rest of the day, she was still so calm. She didn't run or pace the fences like some of the other horses, she seemed content to just stand along the fence and rest. I couldn't take my eyes off her.

Over the next two days my desire to meet Tara close up increased dramatically. It was like she was silently calling me, even though she barely did more than a walk, let alone a call of any kind. As it turned out, Tara was to become my first love.

The first time I needed to serve a mare was an interesting one. Betty and Craig were all prepared, the mare was timed right, they had ropes and a barrier and Betty was even wearing a helmet. Betty was holding the mare through the yard rails and Craig led me around into the entrance of the yard. As soon as I caught whiff of the mare, my manners went out the window. The analogy, 'a bull at a gate'... that was I! What a thrill.

Craig and Betty were in shock at how much preparation they had done, for a situation that became out of control to put it mildly. I just couldn't help myself.

Back Josh came to re-establish my manners and offered to be at the next serving.

I'm not sure though that Josh deserved all of the credit for the second serving being a little more contained... I had known what was coming, as did the mare, so the excitement was slightly more subdued than the first. Nevertheless, I still put on a show for them.

This first season I had just our own mares to serve, the mares at Pleasant Valley that I had known since my arrival, with the exception of Tara.

Tara was the last mare to be served for the season, she had "come in late" I overheard Betty say to a friend on the phone

one afternoon. "I am not even sure she is in a full cycle now." She continued.

"What do you mean, put him in the same paddock as her?" Betty asked into the phone. "I don't know about that... well yes, he has calmed a lot with the process and is quite respectful to the mares. Yes, I have heard it can be better for mares whose cycles we may be unsure of, I'll talk to Craig about it." And she walked off into the house.

A few days went by, then the afternoon arrived that I was to be properly introduced to Tara. Craig came and got me from my yard, as Betty waited in the paddock with Tara. Tara was not on a lead, Betty thought it was best if she was out of the way of any introductions, I felt better about that too, I would never forgive myself if I hurt Betty.

Craig led me into the paddock and kept me on the lead as I moved towards Tara. I stretched out my neck to greet her and she stamped her foot and squealed! I jumped back in surprise. Craig and Betty laughed.

"Oh Shadow you are a softie. Let him loose Craig, they'll be fine I am sure." Betty said, and he let me go. I'd never had a paddock mate before, that's the downside of being a Stallion. But I did have it better than most Stallions I had heard of from the other horses. Apparently most stallions were kept in small boxes, stables, and not allowed out in paddocks at all, let alone with another horse. They had their stable and small yards no bigger than the stable again. How awful. I couldn't imagine it.

I enjoyed my days with Tara, she was a kind mare, and my first real friend outside the farm where I was born. I respected her and always had in mind that I needed to be a gentleman, not like my Father or Grandfather. I was a good horse.

Almost eleven months later, Craig and Betty got the surprise they were dreaming of, when Tara started to show signs of wax on her teats. Betty moved her into the foaling shed, where she would be more comfortable and where the foal would be safer when it entered the world.

Most of the other mares I served had had their foals and Pleasant Valley was certainly a colourful sight. Betty and Craig were so happy with them and me of course. I watched the foals with admiration and admit I was quite proud of my efforts. The foal I really wanted to see though, was Tara's.

The day after Tara was moved into the foaling shed, was when Jameila was born. The first time I saw her she took my breath away. She had almost the same markings as mine, yet her patches were the colour of her mother. She had a gorgeous white strip down her face, just perfect.

Tara was a great mother, she doted on Jameila, and as a result, she quickly grew into a strong young filly. She had her mother's calm nature, but I could tell she had some of my attitude in there too. The look she would give me right before she reared up onto her back legs, flicking her front legs around! That totally gave it away.

CHAPTER ELEVEN

Before we knew it, Summer had passed, and Autumn was upon Pleasant Valley. The trees along the drive had dropped most of their leaves, turning the gravel into a sea of orange and yellow. The mares had started to teach their young independence and the foals were quite happy to play with each other. I remember this time in my life, learning independence, relying on my mother less with each new day.

By the time the next Spring came to Pleasant Valley the foals were weaned from their mothers and had started their halter and lead training. A new type of training routine had also started for me, as Craig and Betty commenced my re-education to the saddle.

I knew what the saddle was, I didn't see the need to go right back to basics. Every day they put the saddle on me and left me in the yard saddled up.

"Patience Shadow, patience is as important as manners," Betty would say each day as she did up the girth.

Spring also brought the start of the show season, and Craig and Betty were eager to get me out into the ring. To be a led horse, they explained I needed to learn to trot along beside them while they ran, trying to stay super straight from my nose to my tail. I enjoyed the challenge at first, but after a week it did start to get boring. I decided to mix it up a little, keep Craig on his toes a bit. Make it a little more exciting. Craig would trot out beside me, so focused, so much concentration on ensuring we were both straight. When I saw him looking straight ahead, I would turn my head and 'nip!'

"Ouch! What the? Betty did you see that?" Craig yelled.

"What happened, did you stumble?" She replied.

"No, the big sod just bit me!" Craig exclaimed. "Watch this."

Craig turned me towards the shed and clicked me up into a trot. I trotted perfectly, the best one of the day for sure. Betty giggled, Craig was annoyed.

Lead lessons were fun with Craig, I loved the anticipation of finding the right moment to sneak in a 'nip' always while Betty could not see. I never hurt him, mostly just got his shirt in my mouth, sure kept him on his toes though!

After each lesson, Craig would complain to Betty, eventually she believed him.

"Well I haven't seen him do any such thing, but if you are concerned, why not lead him in side reins for a bit, keep his head straight." Betty suggested.

The next day I was tacked up with awful side reins. I hated

those things, they reminded me of the horrible time at Sarges and the accident. I didn't mean to hurt him, really I didn't. I lost my balance in them. I had to concentrate to make sure I didn't hurt Craig. I decided to stop nipping him and trot nice and straight like he wanted me to.

The first show we went to was an Agricultural Show, not far from Pleasant Valley. Betty had spent most of the night before washing and drying me, and putting on a soft red show set of rug and hood.

We arrived early and parked away from most of the other trailers and trucks. I think that was the 'done thing' when you had a Stallion. I remember the show I did with Master and his Wife when I was younger. I remembered winning those flappy bits of ribbon. I didn't have to do much training for that show, I just loved to follow Master and his Wife around.

It was different now. I travelled to the show in the trailer alone and had to stand for a much longer time. Betty got me out and tied me to the side of the trailer and proceeded to primp and preen until I fell asleep. She scrubbed my legs again and used clippers to tidy up my fetlocks. My hooves were painted with clear lacquer (which stunk!) and the undersides were cleaned out with a hoof pick and hard brush.

As it got closer to my class, Betty took off the rugs and brushed me all over, then went over again with a sheepskin mitt. I yawned, she laughed.

"Come on Shadow, look excited!" She said.

Excited? We are doing all this again for the chance at a shiny ribbon, I know how this goes. I'd much rather be eating grass. Watching it grow would be more exciting than this.

Betty removed my halter and put on the leather show bridle, she fixed my forelock and did up the throat latch. Craig came around, smartly dressed and thanked Betty as he took my lead, and led me to the arena.

Many of the other exhibitors stopped and looked at us as we entered the arena. They were staring at me I realised. I walked with Craig right out to the middle where our ring was and could hear others whispering and staring in awe.

'Wow, he is something, look at his markings!'

'I have never seen such an impressive looking horse, I can't stop looking at him!'

I gave out a loud neigh in appreciation, a roar as loud as I could and a group of them near me clapped. I knew what they wanted!

Up I went! I stood tall on my back legs, just like I was taught! The crowd around me was in awe, I could hear the wows. Craig pulled my head down and I came to rest again on all fours. I looked over at Betty who had made her way closer to the rings and she was laughing at me, with her hand over her mouth so Craig couldn't see.

Craig clicked me up and we entered our ring. He stood me up for the Judge and I stretched out my neck towards him. The judge walked all around me and then nodded at Craig. Out we went, a big triangle around the ring, coming back to the Judge and halting right in front. We returned to the side of the ring and a blue ribbon was placed on my neck.

The blue ribbon meant I had to go in the ring again, I really just wanted to go home. They all knew I was amazing from my impressive rear, bet none of the other horses could do that. In we went again, and the Judge put a larger ribbon around my neck, a red, white and blue one with gold tassels.

We went to a few more shows after this one and the Judges always put the same coloured ribbons around my neck. At the end of each show we would go home, and Betty would give me carrots as she set me loose in my paddock.

CHAPTER TWELVE

I wasn't interested in the show ring at all, I found it all a bit pointless. But Betty and Craig were excited, and I wanted to make them happy. Because I had done so well at the shows so far, they decided to go big and set their sights on the Australian Championships. The Country's National Show for Arabian Horses and Derivatives.

Aiming for such a prestigious event was a big deal and they researched Trainers who could assist with my preparation. Chellville Training Centre was chosen and the next week I was sent on transport to settle in there and start my show preparation and conditioning.

Chellville Training Centre was a huge establishment. Rows and rows of stables, a large covered area and two round yards. It was run by Jock and Millie, a husband and wife team, with some casual helpers in the afternoons and on weekends.

Jock was a very serious man, a thin wiry build and was always busy. Millie didn't have a lot to do with me, but was very kind whenever she was around my stable. I liked her.

I wasn't myself when I got to Chellville, I was quite nervous and overwhelmed with the amount of other Stallions that were there. They were all quite 'firey' compared to what I was used to. Bold personalities, real showmen I guess. They were all purebred Arabians as well. When they were lead from their stables you could hear them snorting a mile off. They'd snort and prance, with their tails over their back, as if trying to out do each other. It looked exhausting and their energy made me nervous.

The daily routine here was very regimented, I guess it had to be with so many horses needing attention and care. You could time our meals by the sunrise and sunset, and throughout each day the stabled horses took turns having time in the outside day yards.

My conditioning started off slowly, sessions in the round yard at walk and trot and time in the day yards. As I got fitter, I was introduced to the horse treadmill. I hated that thing!

You see, in the round yard I could muck around a bit, sneak in a slow walk, or a pause while Jock wasn't watching. There was no change of pace possible on the treadmill. I was tied to the front, and a barrier blocked me from exiting out the back. The pace was set, and you had absolutely no choice but to keep up. Even if I could slow down somehow, Jock was behind me with a whip, ensuring I didn't slack off.

Did I mention I hated that thing?

It did work, I was getting fitter, but I had no desire to be a super horse. I was quite happy in my stable watching the world go by. I got the impression that it was an important show I was being prepared for.

In between the treadmill and sessions in the round yard Jock worked with me on my show stance. I already knew how to stand! Well, I thought I did. The stance Jock was training me to do was similar, but a lot more extreme and harder to hold. He worked with me until every muscle was working for the stand, my neck was stretching, my body swaying back and forth at the slightest pressure. I could feel every muscle.

Betty and Craig came to check on me one weekend and Millie brought them to the treadmill room where I was working. Jock was behind me with the whip. Betty looked concerned.

"Why is he holding that whip behind him?" She asked.

"Oh, we rarely have to use it, and never use it hard, its just Shadow is a bit well, on the lazy side." Millie laughed. "We thought it may have been his level of fitness, but he tries to get out of work at any opportunity he can."

"I can believe that!" Said Craig, as he looked at me with a grin.

"He does look good though," said Betty, "look at his muscles Craig! He's ripped!"

Jock piped up from the other side of the treadmill. "He's going well, on track for the Championships, just a lazy fella. See how we go."

Jock was non-committal in his tone, Betty got the impression that he wasn't sure about my talent and how I would go at the show. He was used to Pure Arabian Stallions, that he had to hold back, as opposed to encourage forward like me. Prancing around on the end of the lead, compared to me occasionally tripping on a rock.

"We will be proud no matter what he brings home, he looks amazing just now, we are thrilled, thank you" Betty said to Jock and Millie. She turned to me, "You're a good boy Shadow, just try your hardest."

So that is what I set out to do.

CHAPTER THIRTEEN

I knew the Australian Championships were close, as Chellville Training Centre was a bustle of activity. More than usual and routines had changed slightly. Instead of getting two hours in our day yards, we got one hour, and the second hour was spent with the grooms, doing all kinds of treatments. There was clipping, sanding of hooves, pulling of manes, oiling of muzzles and trimming of ears. Every day our hooves were oiled, outside and underneath. I had become a shiny ball of rippling muscle on four legs.

There were twelve of us in the show team. Two other stallions, a younger colt, three mares, four fillies and a gelding. Chellville had a large transport truck, not quite as large as the one that Tara arrived in those years ago, but bigger than most. I hadn't travelled in it yet, but it seemed to carry a lot of horses, as well as rugs and show equipment. There were even cupboards inside that held Jock and Millies show clothes.

The day before the show arrived and we were served breakfast in our stables. By mid morning, the first one, one of the mares, was led to the truck and loaded inside. The other horses followed, including myself and we were on the road, making our way to Toowoomba.

The other stallions snorted and stomped their front hooves with excitement. The young colt mimicked them, except maturity prevented a manly snort, instead a whinny came out. I was never at ease around the other stallions, they tried their hardest to intimidate me at every chance they got. I stood quietly in the safety of my bay, watching the patterns the sun made on the wall as it came through the air vents.

It was a long drive, the longest I had been on, but we eventually arrived at the Showgrounds late in the afternoon.

Jock was driving and found a spot to park alongside a large brick building. It was a long narrow building, like the stables at home, but easily triple the size. Through the vents I could see horses and handlers coming in and out, other people carrying assortments of rugs, wheelbarrows and bins of feed. It was certainly a much bigger show than the others I had been to.

One by one we were led out, down the ramp onto the bitumen road in front of the building. As each of the stallions reached the bottom of the ramp, I heard a loud roar, as they announced their presence to the rest of the grounds. By the time it was my turn, I was impatient with excitement, I was so keen to see more than what the thin line of the vent was showing. Millie came back up the ramp and clipped a lead to my halter and unclipped my trailer tie. Down I went, carefully step by step, right to the bottom of the ramp.

Wow!

The grounds were huge! There were another four brick buildings like the one I had seen through the vent, all the same bricks, but all with their own people and horses going in and out. There were trucks and trailers parked all around, in most every clear spot. Millie led me inside the building and I saw a row of stables either side of the path that went straight down the middle. It was so warm inside and smelt like sawdust and hay. I tried to walk right down the middle of the lane, to stay out of reach of any of the stallions in the other stables. Some had their heads over the doors, craning their necks as if trying to reach me as I passed.

Down we went, around half way down, and into one of the stables. Fresh sawdust, a full bucket of water and an overflowing hay net greeted me as I entered.

"I'll be back a bit later on Shadow, you settle in and relax boy" Millie said as she left the stable, latching the door behind her. I felt safe in my stable.

It was soon nightfall, I only knew this by looking over my stage door and out of the end of the lane way. The building had large lights straight down the middle of the lane way, which illuminated the stables on either side. I heard the rustle of hay bags as other horses grazed. The occasional loud thump made me jump, as someone's hoof connected with their wall. Other stallions asserting themselves by the sound of it. I was eager to watch what was happening in the lane way, as horses came out of the stables to be groomed or rugged, but I didn't want to draw attention to myself. I didn't want the other stallions to force any of their attention on me. They made me nervous and I am sure they knew it. When I got nervous, I instinctively tried to protect myself, and would put my ears back and screw my nose up. When I did this, handlers walking past would move away from the front of my stable.

Morning was indicated by the bustle and chatter of the handlers coming in with the morning feeds. Millie brought my feed in, and changed my heavy stable rugs for a lighter set. One of the grooms came in and raked up my droppings from the night and smoothed out the rest of the sawdust around me, before moving on to the other stables.

After breakfast, I moved to the stable door to watch what was happening outside. There were a few horses tied up on either side of the lane way, getting brushed and having their hooves filed. A group of grooms sat on two bales of hay, chatting and drinking coffee, relaxing after cleaning their allocated stables.

As I craned my neck one of the grooms looked at me and a look of terror came over her face.

"Umm, is that the dangerous horse that went to Chellville?" She said to the others.

"Oh wow, I think it is, look at his markings, not many like him, it must be." Another replied.

Here we ago again, I thought, my 'dangerous horse' reputation. I still don't understand, I tried my hardest to do the best I could and what happened to Sarge was not my fault at all, I was sure it wasn't. I moved back into my stable, and lowered my head to rest.

I was awoken by the latch of the stable as Millie entered and clipped my lead on.

"Come on Shadow, time to go for a walk and stretch your legs before we get you ready!" She said excitedly.

Out we went, out of the stable building and down to a grassy area below. There were four large round yards, each with sand, and they all had a horse in their being worked. Horses snorted and pranced, each showing off to each other and trying to gain the attention of people passing by. I calmly waked beside Millie down to the grass. She loosened the lead and allowed me to graze on the grass. It was so short I had to get my teeth right in there, but it was good to have a fresh pick after being in the stable.

We stayed there for a while, then Millie stroked my neck and said we needed to get ready.

Back in the lane way, I was tied to a ring of twine outside my stable. One of our grooms, Lucy, came and removed my rugs and started to brush me with a super soft body brush. Millie had the best brushes, they must have been very expensive, the bristles were super soft, and they were kept in a separate box to the other grooming tools. Lucy was very kind as well, although I was disappointed she was not with the other grooms while they were discussing my apparent aggressive nature, she would have defended me for sure. She rubbed my face with a warm towel, all around my eyes and nostrils, and then rubbed down my legs.

Next, Lucy retrieved a pin brush, and got to work on my mane and tail. The static electricity in my tail tickled the back of my legs as she went, and I reacted with a big shake of my body. She laughed. The grooming continued, and I was almost asleep when Lucy came around the front to oil my face. I loved this part, Lucy poured some oil on a cloth and would try and concentrate so hard to just get it around my eyes and muzzle. As I felt the cloth touch my face, I would move my head up and down with gusto, rub rub rub! Millie would laugh, and say 'Shadow!' As loud as she could, trying to sound firm, like I was in trouble, but could not hide her laugh. Sometimes I would surprise her with a big rub, that she would half fall backwards, it was so much fun.

After my hooves were painted and make up applied to my face, Lucy went to get Millie. They came back together and put on my show halter, it had the softest leather. I wasn't a fan of the chain, but I guess it was part of that 'show look'. I liked to shake my head up and down to make it jingle. Jock hated it when I did that, but Millie and Lucy just giggled and called me a clown.

The last touch was a sheepskin mitt all over my body, I had developed quite a coat shine these last few weeks, and the sheepskin felt so good.

We walked together down to the arena, Millie leading me, with Lucy following closely behind with a towel, brush and the sheepskin mitt. As we got to the waiting yard, Jock came out of the ring and handed a big bay horse to a groom and came over to us. I instantly sparked up as he grabbed my lead. Jock did not tolerate my laziness, and I was determined to do my best today. I followed him out into the space near the ring entry, and he raised his whip to get my attention. I stood proud and stretched my neck to him, ears pricked.

"Good job mate, you gonna run today?" He sniggered. They knew me well and it did make me wonder how I could have two very different perceptions of me. The people who knew me, knew my laziness, calm nature, but those from the outside saw a dangerous horse. It upset me when I thought about it.

Jock shanked my lead and turned me towards the ring. A couple of other stallions had already gone in, and the man over the speaker called out a number.

'Forty four!" I heard. Jock was wearing a number on the back of his jacket. It must have been forty four, as he moved me forward and we entered the gateway to the ring.

I powered into the ring, showing as much extension in my trot as I could. I could hear the crowd clapping and could feel my muscles ripple as we went right around the arena. We came to a stop on the far side, alongside the other stallions and Jock gave me the command to stand.

Two of the other stallions were palominos, they were a rich light gold colour, like a newly minted gold $2 coin, with a creamy white mane and tail. The others were similar coloured to me, pinto patterns, in varying shades of chestnut and bay.

One by one, we went out in front of the three Judges, displaying our stand, arching and stretching our necks, and then powering around the arena once more. It was hard to hold the stand while three Judges went over me, it took some time, but I did my best.

One of the palominos stood out above the others in the class, he was very impressive. As he was sashed as the winner, I heard the announcer say 'Niarla Amiracle'. He certainly did look like a miracle, a very deserving winner. He strutted his stuff and powered around the arena, the crowd fixed on him. He was sashed as the Australian Champion Partbred Arabian Stallion, and I was awarded Top Ten Australian Champion.

A worthy Australian Champion he was, and as we exited the ring, he gave me a friendly wink and snort. A gentleman as well, I looked up to him after that day. He was only a year older than me but I learnt later that he was technically an uncle to me. His father was the beautiful flaxen stallion 'Amir El Shaklan', who was my Grandfather.

I never got to meet Amir El Shaklan, he was eighteen years of age when I was born, and died in this year, 2006, that Amiracle and I competed in the Australian Championships together. I hoped we made him proud, even if he didn't get to see what beautiful stallions we had become.

Millie and Lucy were so proud of me, and as we made our way out of the ring area, Betty and Craig came running down the hill! Wow! They had come to watch me! I was so happy.

Betty gave me a big hug, and had tears in her eyes.

"Oh Shadow, you clever clever boy! You did so well out there! I am so proud of you!" She was squeezing me so tightly.

"Out with all those other horses, some older than you, wow you did so well! I am so so proud" she continued.
Craig came over and rubbed my face and smiled, "good boy mate, done good." He said. I rubbed him back.

We continued on to the stables, where Lucy and Betty cleaned off my make up, and put my rugs on. They settled me back in with a bucket of feed and topped my water bucket. I was exhausted, so after I had finished my feed, I lowered my head for a rest.

I woke a few hours later to my stable door opening and Betty coming in with a halter and lead. It wasn't one of Chellvilles flashy halters that we had come in, it was a comfortable one that I recognised from Betty and Craig's farm.

"You're coming home now Shadow, you did well. I have missed you so much" Betty said.

Home! I was going home!

Just A Shadow

CHAPTER FOURTEEN

The trailer bounced up the driveway, and I inhaled the familiar smells of Pleasant Valley. I was thrilled to be back home and especially looking forward to seeing Tara.

Craig stopped the truck and Betty came around and lowered the tailgate. Craig untied me and led me out onto the driveway, I arched my neck and tossed my head, eager to stretch my legs in the paddock. The king had come home.

As I turned to head towards the paddock, another horse caught my eye, a horse I had not seen before. I stopped still and gave a loud snort that echoed across the yard.

"Shadow, that is Dancer, he came while you were away." Betty said.

Dancer? Why did they need another stallion? What was this about?

Dancer tossed his head in disgust, I got the impression he wanted to reach me. Who did he think he was? I'd never seen another stallion here at Pleasant Valley that was a pinto like me. Dancer had different coloured patches though, bay and white, with black in his mane and tail. Were they trying to replace me while I was gone?

I stood up to him, I arched neck and roared! This was my home, I was the king here.

"Oh wow Craig, look at Shadow he looks amazing! I have never seen him look so good, quick grab the video camera," I heard Betty say to Craig.

Craig rushed me into the paddock alongside Dancers, and ran to the house to get the camera.

I pranced in slow motion down the fence line, lifting each leg slowly, almost in a piaffe, knees high. Dancer snorted on the other side of the fence, he was no match for me. The mares and young horses in the other paddocks watched in awe at our display.

Dancer and I would never be friends, we always had a rivalry. He didn't understand that it was my home first, all he saw was that I wasn't there when he arrived, and I came later. Every day he antagonised me and I could not ignore it. Some days he would pull faces, ears back and nose screwed up. Other days he would blatantly try to bite me as I grazed near the fence line. I did my best to ignore him, but I was still a Stallion, I couldn't be ridiculed and be seen to take it. I had to show the other horses at Pleasant Valley that I was still the king.

I'd only been home a few months when Craig and Betty decided to start on my re-education under saddle. I had not been ridden since leaving Sarges, and they were cautious about where to start. I'd had such positive experiences since being at Pleasant Valley, they did not want to see me go backwards now.

Craig and Betty chose a local horse breaker, called Marty. Marty had coloured horses of his own and was keen to work with me. He had heard all the rumors about me being a dangerous horse but was prepared to give me a go after speaking with Betty. She was adamant that I was not dangerous, that I had been treated the wrong way. Marty seemed to agree, and was not surprised to learn that I had been taught to rear.

"Well hell, of course that's gonna cause an issue later." I heard Marty say.

Craig and Betty delivered me to Marty's place, and the work started straight away.

For the first few days I was saddled up and lunged in the yard. I had no interest in being lunged, it made me dizzy and I thought it was entirely pointless. Trotting and cantering around in a circle, how ridiculous. Marty would get frustrated by my laziness, but would not let me slack off.

Once Marty realised my lack of motivation to work and saw that I was not reacting to the saddle, he started to put his weight on and off. A few more days and Marty was on my back in the saddle completely. We went right back to basics and spent a lot of time stopping, walking, stopping and walking some more. He was working on making me more responsive, lighter in the aids, as well as listening to his voice commands. I just wanted to stand underneath a tree.

Betty and Craig visited me several times and on the second visit, Marty asked Craig if he wanted to ride me. Craig nodded hesitantly and climbed up on my back.

"He's just an unbalanced horse," Marty said as Craig walked around the yard on me.

"Yeah, he's six years old, but he has never had a chance to build up the right muscles." Craig replied.

"He's lazy, but I reckon a lot of that is lack of strength. He just wants to be a couch potato, because he feels like a couch potato!" Marty said.

Betty laughed. Craig rode me a bit longer, before dismounting and making arrangements to pick me up in few weeks time.

"Ill keep working him every day, get him lighter and more responsive. He's a cheeky bugger, if he thinks he can get out of doing work he will!" Marty said.

The next day Craig put me in the round yard with no saddle. Instead he cracked a whip, and hunted me around the round yard. Faster and faster he made me go, I kept trying to stop, but every time I slowed he would crack the whip towards me.

I was dripping with sweat when he finally allowed me to slow to a trot.

"I'll get you to move yet boy." Marty said. "No horse has beaten me yet."

I wasn't trying to beat him at anything! I just wanted to relax and take it easy in the paddock.

Every day the same happened. Marty put me in the round yard and made me canter around until my heart was pounding and sweat was dripping. Then, he would saddle me up and ride me for another hour. If I tried to slow down while Marty was on my back, he would whack me hard with a wooden paddle that he carried on the saddle.

I tried many times to get him off my back, but it was no use.

After eight days I couldn't take it anymore. My legs were aching from underneath my hooves right up through the muscles in my legs. My lungs felt dry, and my eyes like they could pop out of my head. Marty was on top of me in the saddle, pushing and pushing, whacking me to keep moving, keep the pace, lift my legs. I couldn't take it anymore.

Defeated, I collapsed to the ground in the middle of the round yard and surrendered.

Marty stepped off my back, pulled me up, got back on, and made me walk four more laps of the yard.

Once I accepted the work and just went along with it, I did start to feel fitter, but it didn't mean I liked to do it.

Marty called Betty and Craig to come and get me, and said that he had made me as responsive as he could, but they'd need to persevere with me.

CHAPTER FIFTEEN

I was soon back at Pleasant Valley once more. Unfortunately, Dancer was still there, I don't know why he didn't have to go off and do work round and round a yard getting whacked with a paddle!

Craig continued my saddle work at home, and every second day we could go for a ride in the hills. Betty had said it was to build up my strength. Craig would mix it up a bit and every ride was a little different. A different path up the hill or turning around part way. I always knew when we were headed for home though and I would be thinking of just the right spot to surprise Craig each time.

It made our rides that little bit more interesting and kept Craig on his toes too. When in just the right spot, I would drop my head and kick up my hind legs into a buck. Some times he would fall off, sometimes he wouldn't, but every time he would laugh.

Betty started to watch us on the return as well, she found it amusing, I could see her smile as Craig got up and jumped back on.

Just A Shadow

Betty and Craig liked to joke about how I was 'the dangerous horse'. Really I was just a 'big lazy goofball' Betty would say.

There were many rumors that were spread about me, in addition to being a dangerous stallion. Some folks started rumors that I had the 'wobbles'. The wobbles was a term for a movement disorder in horses. Betty comforted me and told me to ignore anything that I ever overheard.

"Rumors are nothing more than what jealous people wished were true of you." Betty said to me one afternoon.

"You're a unique horse Shadow, you don't realise it. You're more special than you know."

Apparently, I was one of the the highest percentage coloured Arabians in Australia at the time and other breeders were insecure about too many people knowing about me, as it would take services away from their stallions and sales away from their studs.

Kempsey show was my first show under saddle. It was a beautiful sunny day, and I was ready to impress. From the moment I stepped into the warm up area with Craig aboard, I could feel eyes on me. I tried really hard to concentrate and do my best for Craig and Betty.

We won my ridden age class and went in for Champion. The Judge loved me, and after a powerhouse work out, awarded me Champion Ridden Hack. There was a Supreme judging after lunch, so Crag dismounted and gave me a rest in between.

A group of people flooded me, all wanting to say hello and have their chance to pat me and have a photo with my Champion ribbon around my neck. Four ladies who were volunteering for the Red Cross of Australia, came and wrapped their arms around me. Chatting away, they stroked my neck and head.

Next, I was awoken by Craig tightening up my girth. I had fallen asleep! It must have happened while the Red Cross ladies were stroking me, I do remember feeling sleepy, but then the next thing I remembered was Craig tightening up my girth.

Craig climbed aboard and we went back out into the ring to compete for the Supreme Ridden horse of the show. I had no time to wake up properly, it was straight out into the middle of the ring and in front of the Judge.

The pony worked out first, and I watched intently as he flicked his legs around the ring, daintily prancing, neck arched and perfectly manicured tail swishing side to side.

Up a height grouping, and the Galloway moved out in front of the Judge. As if floating on air, the bright bay mare cantered around, as smooth as a rocking horse.

My turn came, and out we went. I tried my hardest, but I just couldn't find the energy I had in the previous classes. I don't know where it had gone.

The Judge awarded the Supreme to the Galloway and the crowd clapped. She walked over to me and said to Craig, "Your horse was my Supreme you know, what happened? Did you forget to set his alarm?" She laughed.

Just A Shadow

A few weeks after the show, earthmoving started at Pleasant Valley. A new riding arena was underway, with a large dozer and an excavator starting the works. A wooden post and rail fence was erected, and the surface of the arena was covered with a sand and dirt mix.

I remember the first time I got to work in the new arena, the surface was so spongey, it was like stepping on elastic clouds.

Betty had a friend called Nessa, and she came to ride me in the new arena every few days. She was fine tuning my dressage skills, and working on my balance. I was developing into a well-trained horse and Nessa enjoyed her rides with me at Pleasant Valley.

When we weren't in the arena, we would explore the trails off the property, I loved to do that. Nessa told Betty I was so bold, so confident out on the trails. Sometimes Nessa would ride Flash and Craig would ride me.

Flash was a gelding who lived at Pleasant Valley, I hated him. He was flaxen in colour and reminded me of my Father and Grandfather. At any opportunity he had he would provoke me into reacting to him and then play scared, so Craig would blame me. Even in separate paddocks he would poke fun of me, running up and down the fence line, antagonising me at every opportunity. I'd arch my neck and strike out, showing him that I was a Stallion and I was not to be messed with. He didn't care, it seemed to give him more motivation to continue. He knew I couldn't actually reach him.

Whenever we were on the trails and Flash got on my nerves

badly, Craig would turn me off the track and point me towards a log. I'd have to think quick and concentrate, it was a good distraction.

Despite my training and fitness routines taking up most of my time, I did still manage to serve mares at Pleasant Valley. Several outside mares had been and gone and some permanent residents of Pleasant Valley would hopefully be expecting as well, including my Tara.

Some mare owners had hesitated to use me initially, because I was not homozygous pinto, meaning that it was not guaranteed I would sire foals that were pinto. They could be solid coloured with no pattern. My mother had the pinto pattern, but had greyed out.

However, it was soon revealed that I threw more coloured foals than solid, even when put to solid mares. Perhaps the best one that was born at Pleasant Valley was Summer. Her mother Jade was a gorgeous bay and Summer was a bay tobiano that took your breath away. Summer was the second foal Jade and I had together, Anastasia was born a few years earlier and looked just like her mother.

Jade was a kind mare, like Tara, but she was a much more dominant personality and enjoyed her own space. I shadowed Tara when we shared the paddock, always grazing along beside her, always in close proximity. Jade had none of that though, and preferred to graze away alone, and just occasionally meet at feed times or near the water trough.

Betty and Craig had planned that I would serve Jade again,

but they didn't seem to be paying attention to her cycles so I decided to take care of it myself. I recognised the signs she was ready, but Betty and Craig had not. I became frustrated waiting, worried I would miss the chance, so one afternoon I jumped three fences to be with her.

When I was found in the paddock with Jade, Betty initially ran screaming, worried I had hurt myself getting in there. When she saw I was fine she scolded me for being so reckless.

However, when Jade presented her with the stunning foal Summer, she silently applauded my efforts.

Summer was the last foal sired by me that was born at Pleasant Valley. Sadly, my time with Craig and Betty was coming to an end. They were desperate for babies of their own, and were travelling to the city a lot to get the help they needed to start their family.

It broke Bettys heart to disband the stud and sell the other horses. I knew it was the hardest decision she had ever had to make in her life. They could not afford acreage near the city, and needed to be close to the doctor and specialists that would hopefully help them produce a family.

"You took my breath away the first time I saw you Shadow, and you never disappointed me once." Betty said to me while feeding up one night. "I will never stop loving you, and I know we will be in touch again someday, I can feel it. You have a future now, a really good one with all you have learnt in your training. You can do anything."

Dancer and the other horses had already been re-homed when I was advertised. Craig said they saved the best for last, Betty said they saved the hardest for last. She really didn't want to let me go. We had been through so much together and grown as a unit.

The first person to look at me was the one who took me home. Trudy. She fell I love with me just as Betty did, I had a way with the ladies.

Trudy wasted no time saddling me up, and putting me through my paces. She had not owned a stallion before. As we rode around the paddock a large plane went overhead. I felt Trudy tense in the saddle, waiting to see my reaction, but I carried on oblivious. It was decided, I would go with Trudy.

Betty cried as I walked up the ramp of the trailer. She was my stepping stone though, a very important piece of my life, which would have been very different without them and everything they taught me.

And that was the end of my life with Craig and Betty. Betty was so sad to watch me go, she was crying. I heard her make Trudy promise lots of things "Look after him please, he really deserves it" and "he is the most remarkable horse".

How I would miss her.

CHAPTER SIXTEEN

Life was very different with Trudy, but a lot of fun. Her home was near the beach, and the air was always warm and fresh. Pickings were slim in the grass department, my paddock was mostly sand, so the grass struggled to grow. But Trudy kept me well fed and I looked forward to burying my head in my feed bucket every night.

Sometimes the rocks hurt my feet and Trudy would allow me to rest in a smaller paddock. Where there wasn't sand, there were a lot of rocks here near the beach. But still, it was nice and warm.

There was no mention of shows or competitions at all. Trudy would tell me that I was a beach horse now and I could just "run around like the 'Black Stallion'!" I didn't know who he was, but sounds like he had a fun life!

The first time I felt the sea breeze was a day I won't ever forget. We walked out onto the sand, it felt so strange. Like I was sinking into the ground. The sand moving under my body weight, it sure took a lot of strength. As we got closer to the water, the sand got harder, more secure. Maybe because it was wet, and the other sand was dry. Trudy told me to "go easy

Boy", as I watched with amazement at the waves crashing before me.

"Its ok, take it easy now, you don't have to go in" Trudy said.

Don't have to go in? Who was she kidding! I was desperate to go in! I boldly walked straight into the water, proving to her how brave and bold I was. I lifted my legs as high as I could, my knees coming up out of the water proud, and my hooves pounding the water.

Trudy giggled, she was having fun too. The waves came up to my chest, almost right up to my back. It felt amazing. I splashed the waves with my hoof, splashing water up onto Trudy. She was laughing now.

"Come on Shadow, that's enough for one day" Trudy said as she turned me around. I bounded out of the waves, in huge leaps! Up and down, through the surf and whitewash, until I reached the sand with a final jump.

Wow. I could handle being a beach horse. This 'Black Stallion' surely did have a fun life if that's what he did!

Trudy had other horses. One of the newer arrivals was a paint mare, who Trudy bought already carrying a foal inside. She was a friendly mare to me, but didn't interact with the others much, she seemed to prefer grazing alone. Her name was Millie.

Millie's foal decided to enter the world during the night. I heard her grunting and stayed near the fence to calm her. I couldn't do much else, I was just there for her. Morning came and revealed the biggest foal I had ever laid eyes on. He seemed to have found his legs pretty quick too! Poor Millie was exhausted and spent the day with her head down and eyes closed. The giant foal would play and jump around the yard, only stopping to steal a drink from his mother, and replenish his energy.

Each day the giant foal seemed to get bigger. He was a muscly thing! Probably because he rarely stopped bouncing around. Trudy would come and feed Millie and try to touch the foal, but he was so naughty, would not let her near him at all. One morning as Trudy was entering the yard, he ran past her at top speed, nearly crashing right into her! Poor Millie did not know what to do with him, he would not listen to his mother.

Trudy was in the garden one afternoon and Mr Naughty was showing off, jumping around the yard and rearing up against his poor Millie. Each time he went past my fence he would build up speed. Trudy just shook her head at him, not game to enter the yard with him carrying on like that. A few minutes later she went inside, the foal was still carrying on. Round and around and around.... when swoosh!! He slid right into the fence and ended up in my paddock!

He jumped up, bewildered, looking at me, back at the fence, and back at me.

"Well!" I sad to him, "what are your plans now?"

"Please don't hurt me Mr Shadow Stallion, please!" He thinks I'm going go hurt him?

"I'm not going to hurt you young lad, even though you really do deserve a talking to. Why are you so naughty every day?" I asked him.

The young foal looked sad. I don't think he knew why he was naughty. I peered over at Millie who gave me a relieved look. This was the first time she'd had a break from her young maniac.

I didn't get any sleep that night, instead I spent the dark hours teaching that foal the right way to behave, how to treat the people and other horses that we come across in our lives. I had his undivided attention, surprisingly, he held onto every word I said.

CHAPTER SEVENTEEN

Birds singing signaled the morning, and I heard the front door open and Trudy come out of the house. She screamed! I jumped! What was wrong with her? She bolted to my paddock and jumped the fence to come beside me.

"Oh Shadow! How did this happen? How did he get in here? Have you hurt him?" Trudy said in a panicked voice.

Hurt him? I scoffed to myself... why does everyone think that, because I'm a Stallion? Well I am NOT like my Father or Grandfather. I walked over to the foal and pushed him forward with my muzzle, towards Trudy. Trudy gaped in amazement as the foal came towards her. She reached out her hand and the foal looked at me. I nodded in encouragement and he stepped closer to her, allowing her to place her hand on his head. Trudy was shocked, so shocked, that she left that naughty creature in my paddock!

"Well, you're due to be weaned now anyway, so I guess this is it? Let's see how this goes."

The only one that looked happier than Trudy was Millie.

I spent my days teaching that foal all I knew. How to respect humans, as the quality of life we have directly depends on them. The poor naive little fellow had no idea what I meant. Someday you may end up with a human who may not like you, or may not place an importance on giving you the best care they could. You need to try and avoid this type of home all you can, and you do that by being a good horse. Never scare or hurt a person, or they will be afraid and send you away. Try and understand them, people love it when you look like you are interested in their babble.

As the months went by Grasshopper, as I had affectionately named him, became a fine young colt. Every now and then his confidence would get the better of him, and I would need to remind him of his place. I never hurt him though, not like my Father and Grandfather hurt me. I cared for the young fellow and wanted to teach him with kindness, not force. He responded to this and loved to show off his new skills in front of Trudy.

Trudy would laugh, then come over to me and whisper "You're a gentleman Shadow, thank you."

Soon it was time for Grasshopper to learn about a halter and lead. I saw Trudy come from the gear shed with a halter and long rope. I walked over to Grasshopper and explained what was about to happen.

"This is a very important lesson my young charge, how you respond to this challenge will shape your future. If you react badly and hurt Trudy, things may not end so well for you I am afraid. I need you to be brave now and accept the halter that will be placed upon you." He snorted at me.

Just A Shadow

Oh brother, I sighed.

"I am being very serious now! I have not wasted this time on you prove to me you are sensible and brave."

Grasshopper nodded, and walked towards the halter which was now hanging over the gate. He sniffed it, and jumped back. I rolled my eyes, and gestured back at the halter with my nose. He took another step back towards it, and had a good long sniff this time. I walked over to him and winked my approval.

"Now, help me out Shadow, should I put this pocket rocket in the small yard to tackle this?" Trudy asked me. She was always asking me for advice, about her life, her friends, and her husband. I could never answer her, but it seemed to reassure her just to have my listening ear.

I grabbed the halter in my mouth and walked it over to her. She laughed.

"You want me to put it on him here? In this huge paddock?" She laughed louder this time. I nodded. Trudy eyes went a little wider. She looked at Grasshopper and looked back at me.

Grasshopper was standing quite close to me and did not seemed concerned. Trudy pulled the halter from my mouth and stepped towards him.

Well I'll be. That naughty little foal lowered his head, and pushed his nose into the halter. I was very proud.

Trudy continued to slide the rest of the halter up around behind his ears and do up the cheek buckle, all the while Grasshopper stood still. Trudy rubbed her hand up and down his neck, telling him he was a very good boy. She then went and got us both a big bucket of grain mix.

Trudy left Grasshopper to become used to wearing the halter before she put the lead on. Every morning and every night she fed us both together and Grasshopper allowed her to rub his neck, and all over his body with a soft brush. He had turned into a very respectable colt and I think even Trudy enjoyed the training process.

When the time came, Grasshopper accepted the lead just as well. He fell asleep during his tie up lesson and followed Trudy like a puppy when learning to lead. He progressed so well through all the stages and soon it was time to find his next home. He was excited about seeing new places and getting to know his next family. I couldn't be more proud of him.

It did not take long for Grasshopper to be secured by his next home. The first man that looked at him adored him and praised Trudy for how she had instilled his early training. I heard Trudy say "I wish I could take all the credit, but that coloured horse over there... it was all him."

"But he is a Stallion? This colt was in with him?" The man asked surprised.

"Yes, he was, and Shadow gave him a future."

CHAPTER EIGHTEEN

After Grasshopper went, Trudy seemed to worry that I was lonely. I heard her talking Bob (her husband in the big house) and she sounded like she wanted him to let her get me a friend. A friend would be great I thought, but I never really had a friend that lived in the same paddock as me.

"Please Bob!" I would hear Trudy shout, "he is such a lovely boy, he would love a friend! I can't bear to have him here all alone, he looks so sad."

I wasn't sad, I didn't have much to do when Trudy went to work though, so a friend could be interesting. I would wait and see what happened. I wonder what a friend looks like?

One morning, I was quietly resting under one of the beach trees at the far end of my paddock, when I saw Trudy leave with the horse trailer. I wondered if we were going somewhere for a ride! Trudy often took me in the trailer to new places. It was great to ride through tracks we hadn't been before and see different animals. I started to trot up towards the drive way.

No, Trudy drove right out the gate! Where was she going without me? I didn't understand. Was I naughty last time we went out? I didn't think I was. Oh, I hope I had been a good boy. I walked back down to the corner of my paddock and put my head down near my legs. Sigh, I hope she comes back soon.

It was one of the longest days I remember. I thought of Trudy all day. Wondering where she had gone, why did she take the empty horse trailer… I didn't understand.

As the sun started to set, I wandered up to the fence that followed the drive way, to wait for my dinner. I hoped Trudy would come back soon. And then, as if my thoughts made it happen, Trudy's truck came rattling up the drive, with the horse trailer towing behind.

I gave an excited snort as she came closer, eager to find out where she had been. I saw Trudy in the driver's seat and she gave me a pleased smile as she continued on to park the truck and trailer.

The area that Trudy used to help me on and off the horse trailer was not visible from my fence. I craned my neck as far as I could, stretching it far over the fence trying to see around the feed shed. Argh, I could not see what she was doing.

I heard the tail gate of the horse trailer drop onto the drive way, and soon after I heard…. hooves? Hooves? Someone was getting out of the horse trailer?

I waited with anticipation, so frustrated that I couldn't see… I called out! I heard Trudy laugh "Shadow, be patient, we are coming!"

We? We? It was another horse!

Around the corner walked the most beautiful mare I had ever seen. My eyes locked on her and she blinked her deep brown eyes back at me. I was instantly in love. Trudy and the mare came closer and Trudy allowed me to sniff the mare over the fence.

"Shadow, this is Scarlett and she is going to be your friend and share your paddock."

I couldn't believe it, she was going to be with me in my paddock? She was amazing, a rich red colour, with the blackest of black mane and tail. Her legs were black and shaded up into the red colour of her body. Her muzzle had the same black, and faded up into her cheeks. Right down the middle of her face, a stark white stripe. She was perfect. My Scarlett.

Scarlett nuzzled against my cheek. Trudy walked her around to the gate, I followed eagerly, I could not take my eyes off her. As she came through the gateway, I stepped to the side, like a gentleman and allowed her space to come through. I was determined to be a better stallion than my Father and Grandfather, in all respects. Scarlett arched her neck in appreciation and skipped into a rhythmic prance. I followed, like a big puppy whose child had run off with their ball to play. Besotted.

The days were so much more enjoyable with Scarlett by my side. I still got to go for trips with Trudy to explore, but Scarlett would stay behind. She didn't mind though. She told me that she enjoyed the space and the quiet while I was on my adventures. I did like to be her Shadow. Trudy would tell me to give her space, as she was older than me, and would sometimes prefer to rest alone, get her beauty sleep. I knew she didn't need any beauty sleep though, she was perfect. Inside and out. The sweetest mare, I would often stare at her while she watched the birds high up in the trees. She especially loved the Black Cockatoos that would occasionally visit. They were large birds, and only visited every now and then, so when they appeared it was a sight indeed.

"They signal rain it is thought," Scarlett said to me one day.

I was fascinated, what clever birds. When they flew, you could see bright red feathers underneath their wings.

One afternoon Trudy and I were on a ride down near the beach and Trudy started to talk to me about Scarlett. She told me that she had brought her to be with me, in the hopes that we may have our own foal together one day.

"She is a very valuable mare Shadow, I did not pay a lot for her, I am not sure why, but as a younger horse she was sold for $10,000." Trudy explained. "You will know when the time is right, I can tell how much you love her."

Wow, I thought to myself, I wonder why Trudy didn't have to pay that much? It didn't matter though, Scarlett was with me for good and I would try my best to make a beautiful foal with her, to care for and raise into the world. I yearned for the chance to raise a foal that was my very own son or daughter and a foal that had Scarlett as their mother was sure to be exquisite.

Scarlett and I enjoyed spending time together, but the idea of a foal together seemed to be slipping. Scarlett would allow me to try, but then months later when the Vet would check, there would be no foal growing inside her. Trudy was so sad. The vets visited a lot, but they just didn't know why Scarlett could not grow a foal.

"That's why she was so bloody cheap!" I heard Trudy say on the phone once. She was very sad. I hoped that Scarlett was not going to get in trouble or not be allowed to stay.

But, Scarlett stayed, and I was so relieved. I didn't mind that she couldn't make a foal, it meant that I got all of her attention. I adored her regardless and hoped that we would be together forever.

Trudy stayed sad for a long time after this. At first, I thought she was so sad because she wanted us to make a foal so bad, but it was much more than that. Trudy had other things going on in her life, with her husband and other things. She came to me one afternoon, and her face was wet, her eyes red.

"Shadow, I am so sorry." She whispered to me as she placed her hands on either side of my face. My ears pricked, I didn't understand. "I have to find you a new home."

What? No! This could not be happening! I don't want to go to a new home, I can't leave Scarlett!

"I wish with all my heart I could keep you, but I just can't. I need to get away from this house, and I have tried to find a paddock for you to stay in, but no one wants to have a stallion on their property. I promise I will try and find you a nice person, a person who will love you like I have, hopefully even a lady person. You are such a gentleman, you need to find a lady to care for you." Trudy was crying more now. She held me a little longer, and walked back up to the house.

We did not go for any rides out after that, Trudy seemed too sad to think about rides. I didn't mind, I was so worried about soon not having any more time with Scarlett. I wanted to spend every second I could with her.

A few weeks passed by, and then Trudy's phone seemed to be keeping her very busy. Most often she was talking about me. I would try and listen, but it was hard to understand a conversation that you can only hear one side of. Sometimes the phone calls were short, and sometimes they went a little longer. I overheard Trudy on one phone call that got my ears pricked.

"Where did you say you were?" Trudy asked into the phone. "Abu Dhabi? Are you serious? I don't even know what is involved in that, he would have to go on a ship or a plane?"

A plane? Those big noisy things that flew overhead? I started to feel scared.

"No, I am sorry. I just can't put him through that. I don't think I can sell him to you." Trudy said down the phone.

Phew!

Most of the phone calls seemed to end in a similar way. Trudy asking lots of questions, and then politely telling the other person that they were not the home for me. I appreciated that she wanted the best for me.

A week went by and the phone calls seemed to stop. Until one afternoon while preparing feed for Scarlett and I, Trudy's phone rang.

I listened with a half ear as Trudy answered. "Yes, he has always been a ladie's horse, he is very kind" Trudy said to the caller through the phone. "He was my first Stallion, I had never owned an entire male before him and I was hesitant too!" She laughed.

Trudy had not laughed in a long time. Not since she told me that I would be leaving her for a new home in the future. Whoever was on the other end of the phone must be making her feel happy.

"Yes, there are several places to stay if you came up the night before", Trudy continued, "I look forward to meeting you."

That was the call that was to turn my life in new direction.

CHAPTER NINETEEN

I wasn't sure when to expect my visit from the mysterious lady, but when I saw Trudy near the gate raking leaves I guessed it was going to be soon. Sure enough, only an hour later a truck towing a horse trailer came down the drive.

Gee, I thought, keen aren't they! Bringing a trailer all this way, don't I get a say in whether I like them or not? And I am really not keen to go anywhere without Scarlett.

I watched as the man and woman got out of the truck and walked down to see Trudy. They talked for a while, then came over to see me. I pretended I couldn't see them, and pushed my nose through the grass pretending to graze.

"Shadow! Shaaadddooooww" Trudy called. "Oh he is a sod, look at that ignoring me, selective hearing like a child!"

The lady laughed. My ears pricked and I raised my head to look at her. She had the most unique laugh I had ever heard. A laugh like no other I had heard before. I started to wander down to the gate, the lady laughed again at something her husband said, and I picked up into canter... I had to meet her.

Just A Shadow

The laughing lady's name was Abby, and her husband was Bruce. They had driven nearly a full day to see me, that's why they brought the trailer, a big trip to do another if they did like me. Bruce was the first to say hello, he stroked my forehead, for a man he was very gentle. He looked into my eyes, like he was trying to see inside. I nuzzled his chest and he smiled. I got a good feeling from him.

Bruce turned back to join the conversation. "Abby is the horse mad one, I am a cattle farmer. She is spending a fortune on stallion fees and traipsing her mares all over the country side. It was my idea to come up and look at this guy. Makes sense to have a Stallion, but we have never owned one before. Abby has handled plenty, but never had one at home."

Abby. The laughing lady.

"Well let's say hello to Shadow, shall we?" Trudy said and grabbed my halter and lead. She took me to the arena and put me through my paces on the lunge. I showed off a little, I really liked them and wanted them to think I was amazing. I jumped up in the air, I showed my best extended trot and I showed them my beautiful neck arch while collecting my movement. I looked over to see how impressed they were.

Bruce did not look real excited, he said "He is nice, but how quiet is he? He doesn't seem very quiet."

"Oh, he is truly sensible I promise, he must just be feeling fresh." Trudy replied.

Bruce came into the arena and stroked my neck. "I have to be sure I can trust you old mate, I care about Abby very much, and need to know you are sensible enough to look after her."

I breathed a sigh of relief. He didn't care about my show results, my big movement or how I looked... he just wanted to know I wouldn't hurt Abby. I walked back over to the gate where she was standing and snorted quietly. Abby walked over and I sniffed her very gently. I closed my eyes while she stroked my face. Her hands ran over my closed eyes. It was heaven.

"Ok, we will take him" Bruce said. Abbys hands squeezed my face a little, and I rubbed her in acknowledgment. Bruce and Trudy went to talk money, and Abby stayed with me.

Being close to Abby was so nice I didn't notice Scarlett come down to the gate. "Oh hello sweet girl" Abby said, "you are beautiful." Scarlett nickered.

I walked over and Scarlett buried her nose in my mane.

"Oh, you are friends aren't you," Abby said. "Oh dear."

Bruce and Trudy had just finished talking, and Bruce made his way to the trailer to put down the ramp. Trudy clipped my lead back on, and started to pull me towards the gate. I was torn! I couldn't leave Scarlett, but I didn't want Abby to go without me!

Bruce walked over and told Abby he was ready to load me up. Abby looked concerned.

"Trudy, the mare there with Shadow, who is she?" Abby asked.

Just A Shadow

"That is Scarlett, she is Shadows paddock mate. I bought her in the hopes of a foal but she never produced. She sold for $8500 as a younger horse, but I am afraid her only worth now is as a companion." Trudy explained.

"Oh Bruce, we can't leave her, this will break my heart" Abby said to Bruce.

He laughed. "Abby we came here for one horse, not two!"

"But two will fit? And he will travel better with a friend? And settle better at home with a familiar friend" Abby said.

Bruce seemed to know that any objection would be tiring, so off Trudy went to get another halter and lead, and soon, Scarlett and I were on our way, together.

CHAPTER TWENTY

The trip to our new home was very long, we went through many towns I had never seen before. Over bridges, through winding mountains, and through a huge city. Sydney, I heard a passer by say when we had stopped. Bruce and Abby stopped often to check on us, Abby would offer us food and water, but we did not get out of the trailer. The roads seemed far too busy and noisy. Scarlett slept standing up most of the way, I was too excited.

At one set of traffic lights that we stopped at, a bunch of Chinese people all leaned out and were saying words to me and taking photos! I did my best Shadow snort, and they loved it. All I heard was camera shutters. Abby saw this through her side mirror and smiled.

Eventually we arrived at our new home.

It was a beautiful big farm, huge gum trees provided cool shade and there were lots of dams for our water.

Bruce led me out of the trailer first. I couldn't believe the feel of the soft grass. No sand or rocks. It was like walking onto clouds, not that I knew what that felt like, but I imagined clouds to be pretty soft! The breeze filled my nostrils, it was so fresh.

Scarlett followed behind with Abby and as her hooves touched the ground her eyes went soft. She felt it too. She rubbed Abby's arm in appreciation.

"Let's just keep them on the lead a bit, let them get their bearings," Abby said to Bruce.

They walked both of us around, through into the next paddock, which seemed even bigger than the one we just drove through.

As well as being so dreamingly soft, the grass tasted so good too. I didn't want to lift my head, and when I heard Abby's laugh and turned, I saw Scarlett wasn't keen to lift her head either.

Bruce and Abby removed our halters and set us both free. It felt like nothing I had ever felt before. I had never been in a paddock so big, so natural, so many trees. I wanted to run and jump and explore, but I was conscious of being a gentleman and so I walked alongside Scarlett and we explored our surrounds together.

CHAPTER TWENTY ONE

Abby spent time with Scarlett and I every day. There were small children in our new family as well. I had never seen these small people up close before. They were very fast. They would run around and around, and Abby would shout at them to 'come back' and 'don't go down there!' but then she would laugh, and the small people would laugh back at her.

A few days after we arrived Abby was pottering around, brushing Scarlett, when her phone rang.

"Yes we bought him, he is lovely!" she said to the person on the phone. "No I don't have a stable… no not a small yard either, why?"

"Oh that's crazy!" Abby laughed into the phone, "He is in a 30acre paddock now, and he is standing right beside me while I brush Scarlett. Its ok Melinda."

Melinda? Who trained me for my big shows? That was so long ago, I still remembered her though. I think she was telling Abby that I shouldn't be in such a big paddock.

"Honestly he is fine, but thank you so much, maybe he has

changed since then? He doesn't seem to want to leave me while I am in here with him and he certainly hasn't tried to attack me or Scarlett!"

I was a sad and misunderstood horse in my early days. Melinda must have been telling Abby about me not liking the other Stallions. I knew I was different now, I promised myself and Bruce that I would not hurt anyone, especially Abby, and I meant it.

Scarlett and I had no pressures here with Bruce and Abby and their small children. We spent our days grazing on the soft grass and standing in the shade while the breeze went through our tails. There weren't a lot of other horses, mostly cows and they didn't seem to mind us at all, so I didn't mind them.

Over the fence on one side of my paddock there was a big old chestnut horse, a Thoroughbred. He was very tall, but I could tell his poor body had seen better days. He must have been almost 30 years old or more. He didn't wander around much. His people were old too. They weren't young like Bruce and Abby. Hazel was a lovely old lady, she was often outside letting her chickens in and out and would gaze over at me. Adam was her husband, he was in charge of the cows and spent a lot of time walking through the paddocks checking on them, and any new calves that had been born.

Life was good here, we had amazing views from our paddock, we could see so much. There were mountains off in the distance, with cliffs that turned bright orange as the sun hit them in the afternoons.

Kookaburras cackled away throughout the day and super fast little rabbits raced between the blackberry bushes. The occasional echidna would stroll past us at a leisurely pace, and there was a family of wild ducks that chose our dam as their home.

Scarlett loved it just as much as I did. Her favorite place was the big tree near the gate, it gave us a lot of shade and was higher than the rest of the paddock, so the view was even better.

The first time Abby and Bruce had a job for me, was a very funny experience. I had overheard that I was the first Stallion for Abby, and I knew she had been 'researching' how she should go about it. I wanted to tell her that she didn't have to worry, I knew what I was doing.

Abby came and got me from the paddock, and led me down to the wooden yards. Bruce was there waiting, holding a beautiful bay mare through the rails. As well as the halter and lead, Abby had put an Anti-rearing bit in my mouth. She was also wearing a helmet. I think she thought I was going to turn into a raging Tyrannosaurus Rex at the first sight of a mare, and somehow end up on top of her. I was a little amused.

As we came around to the gate of the yards, I started my fancy dance for the mare. I was snorting and prancing on my toes, my neck arched in a display of masculinity. I entered the yard, slowing to a piaffe, on the spot, then stopped. I stretched my neck forward towards the mare, out of the corner of my eye I could see Abby's eyes were wide. She was holding the lead loose to allow me to stretch forward, but I was sure she was ready to leap out of the way at any second!

My nostrils grew wide... I leaned forward as far as I could....

No.

"Ummm, Shadow?" Abby said, "what are you doing? Why have you stopped?"

She really had no idea. You see the mare was not ready. And when a mare isn't ready, they are not going to let things go any further, trust me! Abby didn't seem to understand this.

"Shadow! Go! Look!" She yelled, tugging on my lead and pointing at the mare.

Oh brother. I planted my feet, there was no way I was putting myself in the line of those unwilling hooves in front of me!

Abby muttered some words and told Bruce it was pointless. She begrudgingly led me back to my paddock, with no idea that I had just saved us both from the force of some unhappy back legs!

It wasn't the last time Abby thought she knew best. She had her bits of paper, with charts drawn on them and was forever checking mares and writing things down. I would watch her do the rounds, writing and writing, and snicker to myself.

Eventually she got sick of her bits of paper and gave up. Bruce suggested just putting the mares in with me, "because that's how the bulls did it". Abby thought that was ridiculous at first, but realised she was getting no where with her charts.

The first mare she put through into the paddock with Scarlett and I was Monalisa. She was a beautiful mare, a pure Arabian, with a bright bay coat and pitch black mane and tail. She was quite tall and had an exquisite face. Monalisa lived with us for a few months, and I did my job when the times were right.

Abby affectionately nicknamed me "Mr Clooney", as I was so gentle and loved all of my mares.

Being such a fine mare, it didn't take long for Monalisa's growing belly to become obvious, Abby was ecstatic.

Monalisa was moved to another paddock to grow her baby.

CHAPTER TWENTY TWO

Months went by and it was getting close to her due date. Abby spent the nights sleeping by the wooden yard, with a whole load of bits and pieces. She really thought none of us knew what we were doing! Sweet Abby.

One afternoon Abby had gone to fetch the children, Jolene and Hannah, from school. Monalisa decided it was her time. I watched eagerly from my paddock, the miracle of birth. Monalisa did an amazing job and adored her baby as soon as she saw her. A gorgeous coloured filly, a mini me almost, with long legs like her mother.

Scarlett joined me at the fence line and we watched together as the foal tried to stand. Up, up, up, up.... nope. This went on, until... yes! She had it. A very strong foal, she was standing in no time at all, and searching for that warm milk bar.

I glanced at Scarlett, you could almost say she looked a little sad. I don't know why she couldn't have foals of her own any more, but I did know something. "Congratulations Grandma" I said, "you're going to be the best one ever." Scarlett nuzzled my face.

Abby arrived back, and leaped out of her car when she saw the extra legs in the yard. She ran as fast as she could over to the yard, and stared gaping at the new foal.

"Wow." Was all she could manage to say.

Abby named the new foal Khaleesi, and she was besotted with her. The filly certainly got her handling early! Abby and the children adored her. Every afternoon they would feed Monalisa and play with Khaleesi.

Some afternoons if Khaleesi had had a big day, she would lay down while Monalisa grazed, and Hannah would sit next to her on the ground. I watched from my paddock as the mutual respect and admiration glowed from both of them. Abby wanted her children to love and respect animals and they were certainly showing they were on the right path.

By the time Khaleesi needed to be weaned, there was nothing I could offer. She was already handled by the constant attention and was sure to make a fine horse as she grew. I was sure she was destined for a good future and was very proud.

Khaleesi was introduced to Malii and put into the paddock with her. Monalisa accepted the process as well and was eager to get out into the large paddock again.

Malii was Abby's grey mare. She was a show horse in her younger days, like I was. She was a Show Champion and was undefeated for her beautiful classic Arabian head. These days she spent her time grazing on the highest hill on the farm, overlooking the world. Malii became a good teacher for

Khaleesi. The filly mimicked everything Malii did.

Malii was definitely the 'Alpha mare' at the farm, but she was not mean or aggressive. All of the foals just knew she was the boss, like a stern aunty and they respected her.

I enjoyed the days where I could see Bruce working out in the paddocks. When I couldn't see him, I could hear the familiar growl of the truck in the distance. He would often drive through the gullies, checking the cattle and the bull.

I enjoyed having the old gelding as company through the quiet months, he did not say a lot, or move around much, but he was always there grazing along my fence line.

The winters were cold on the farm. Frost lined the paddocks in the mornings and the dams displayed a thin layer of ice. As the frost along the wire fences melted, spider webs would sparkle and glisten with the coming up of the sun.

I didn't see much of the children during the colder months, only the occasional weekend where they would join Bruce collecting firewood. I loved to watch them play. They would run up the hills and roll back down again, laughing and giggling.

The birds seemed to fly somewhere else to avoid the cold I assumed. Their absence was noticed by the quiet mornings void of their usual song and chatter. The colony of rabbits that lived amongst the blackberry bushes were not slowed by the weather however, and each day they hurried about between the bushes, leaping and bounding in a hurried frenzy of activity.

Khaleesi was growing into a beautiful yearling, even through her thick winter coat I could see she was going to be a fine mare one day.

The return of the birds signaled that winter was almost over, and the days seemed to get longer once again. The farm became a hive of activity once more with Bruce moving cattle between paddocks and fixing fences. Abby was also around the yards more, and had started to do some handling lessons with Khaleesi.

Even the old gelding seemed to perk up a little, and wander around his paddock more.

"Are you ready for the new season Shadow?" Abby said one morning as she was doing her rounds checking on all of the horses. "We have some lovely mares planned for you and maybe even Monalisa again, we just adore Khaleesi, you did so good."

I snorted my appreciation, and pushed Abby with my head.

Abby certainly had planned the season for me and the first mare to arrive was Kay. She was not an Arabian like most of the other mares who visited me at the farm, she was much more solid, and had exquisite markings, overo they were called.

Kay had been a successful show horse, in the Western arena and was known as 'Love is in the Air', and it was. I fell in love with her as soon as I saw her.

Bruce put her in my paddock not long after she arrived, and we enjoyed our time together. Bruce would drive into the paddock with hay on the back of his Ute, and Kay and I would share our meals. I respected her, she was such a calm mare, she had seen a lot of the world. Kay had won several National Champion awards, under saddle and at halter before she sustained an injury which stopped her career. She had torn a ligament in her front leg, thought to be caused by stress to her growing legs from competing under saddle at such a young age. She had found a nice life now though, her owners Kerryn and Rick were lovely and were very excited at us sharing a paddock.

Scarlett was not far away, she had gone for a little holiday up at Grandma's place when the mares had started to arrive for the season.

Grandma was a funny old lady, she was Bruce's mother Abby had told me. She lived not far from our farm. Grandmas paddocks were full of grass, and she had no horses there to enjoy the pasture. So Bruce said that Scarlett could stay there with Grandma and keep her company for a few months.

Other mares came and went throughout the Spring, and Bruce and Abby were so proud of me. Abby trusted me to know when the mares were ready, and in turn I respected her and allowed her to move the mares around the farm without fuss or call from me.

Kay and I roamed the paddock alone, after the other mares had been served and collected by their owners. We took shelter amongst the thick trees on the farm, it was the most comfortable and relaxed I had felt my entire life.

CHAPTER TWENTY THREE

On the days Bruce came to check the cows, he would drive into the paddock with Kay and I, with biscuits of lucerne hay on the back of the truck. Kay and I would graze together peacefully, in no rush at all.

Kay stayed the rest of Spring and all through Summer. It was almost Autumn when Kerryn and Rick arranged for her to come home to prepare for her last few months of pregnancy. I was sad to see her go, and hoped I would see her again.

After she had gone, Abby surprised me with Scarlett and I was thrilled to have her company again. I never liked being alone, I heard most other stallions were kept alone, and weren't allowed to share their paddocks with anyone else. How awful that must be. Scarlett enjoyed our time together as much as I did.

As the weeks went on through the Autumn months, I noticed that Abby was getting bigger as well, around her belly, it was growing. She came into the paddock to check on us one afternoon, and I gently nuzzled her stomach. She laughed.

"I am having a baby too Shadow," Abby told me, "Bruce is excited too."

Abby and Bruce already had two little people, and now a third one was coming, love was blossoming on our farm.

Autumn turned into Winter and I saw less and less of Abby. She was slower around the farm, and took longer than usual to get in and out of the truck. I missed her visits, but understood she had to rest.

Scarlett and I spent the days around the lower parts of the farm, in the gullies where the trees provided shelter from the wind. It was peaceful, we had not a worry in the world.

A new horse arrived one afternoon, driven by Bruce in his truck and trailer. A funny looking colt with a huge head and big thick white blaze and four long white stockings up his legs. The stockings were fluffy, covered in thick tufts of hair called feathers. He had hooves like dinner plates.

"This is Fred Shadow, he will be alongside your paddock, teach him some manners eh?" Bruce said. "He's gonna be a big boy that's for sure. Maybe I'll get him pulling a cart or a plough one day, bit of fun, always wanted a Clydesdale."

For the winter months, Bruce had opened up a lot of the gates on the farm, so separate paddocks had become open passageways. The cattle shared these paddocks with us, and we enjoyed watching them graze with their young heifers from the year before, moving through the farm in lines, following each other closely.

As the weather warmed, the farm again showed more activity. Rabbits, and lots of small additional rabbits, again filled the paddocks with hustle and bustle.

Bruce always spent the first few weeks of the new season checking fences for any broken spots which were usually either caused by fallen trees or kangaroos. If he stopped near us to fix a spot, Scarlett and I would wander over to keep him company. He seemed to like us being near, as long as I didn't move any of his tools around, or try and push him over while he was banging in a post.

Fred would pace up and down his fence line, annoyed he couldn't join in the fun too. He had no idea of his size though, in just a few months he'd grown almost another hand.

Jolene and Hannah occasionally joined Bruce on his jobs around the farm, but Abby hadn't come for a while. I missed her and hoped she was ok. Maybe she had her baby? Was that why she had not come out in the paddock?

I didn't have to wonder for long as a few days later Abby arrived, with a special little bundle in blanket. Bruce took the bundle and Abby raced over to my fence. My ears pricked and I eagerly pushed my chest against the gate, stretching my neck as far as I could towards her. She got to the gate and wrapped her arms around my neck. Scarlett came up for a pat too.

"Oh I missed you guys," Abby said. "Kay had her baby too! She had a beautiful filly, who looks just like her, same colour and same markings. You did well Shadow, she is beautiful. They called her Smooch, no surprises where that name came from she must be like you in that regard!"

A filly, I bet she was beautiful and I bet Kay was as good a mum as Abby was as well. Bruce walked over, and moved the blanket off the babies face.

"This is James Shadow," he said. I carefully moved towards him and had a little sniff. He looked just like Bruce.

Little James slept a lot, which meant Abby could walk around the paddocks with the girls and spend time with all of us. James seemed to enjoy being with Bruce, and Bruce was besotted with him. A father and his son, it was something to see and admire.

One afternoon Bruce and baby James were over near the road fence, straining up some loose spots. Abby was at the shed with Jolene and Hannah and she came out with my bridle.

"Jolene can you help me sweety?" She asked.

"What are you doing mum? You can't ride Shadow, Dad will be mad if you ride you know." Jolene said.

Abby used to be a great rider I had heard. Amongst the gear there was saddlecloths that had logos of feed companies on them, that sponsored her to compete and promote their food. There were also rugs that had names of awards on them. I often wondered why she didn't ride anymore, but thought it was just because she was busy with the children all the time.

"Dad just freaks out because I freak out, I used to ride a lot you know before you were born. Having kids changes you somehow, just don't have the nerve I used to." Abby replied.

She pulled the bridle up over my nose, and did up the straps. She passed the reins over my neck, and Jolene held them down near the bit. Abby grabbed a milk crate, and with one swift move, was on my back.

"Ok sweety, I'm just going to do a circle, look after me now Shadow." Abby said nervously.

I did.

We walked a circle, and I could tell Abby was relaxing. She asked me to walk some more. I was the King of the valley and Abby was my Queen rider, I was her sturdy protector.

"What the! Abby!" Bruce yelled.

"Uh oh, busted Shadow!" Abby giggled. "I better get off now."

I walked her over to the shed and she slid off. She took off my bridle and gave me a big hug. I could tell she enjoyed our ride.

Bruce arrived beside us. "What the hell were you thinking? Just jumping on like that out of the blue!"

"It's ok Bruce," Abby replied, "I had to do it that way. If I thought about it too l long, I'd psych myself out of it."

"I understand, but really Abby, in a 50acre paddock with no saddle?" Bruce sighed.

Abby smiled at me. We had a special bond, and she knew it too.

CHAPTER TWENTY FOUR

It must have been just after midnight that I first heard the old geldings painful groan. He had grown tired over the last months, more so than usual, and would barely move more than a few metres throughout each day. Dam, to tree, and back to dam again in the afternoon.

I walked over to the fence line, and tried to see through the darkness. I could vaguely make out the shape of his body in the moonlight, laying down. I called to him, and he turned his head slightly in my direction.

He was done.

As sad as death is, sometimes you have to appreciate it. You have to appreciate it when it happens calmly and at the end of a full life. I am unsure exactly how old he was, but his arthritis and grey whiskers indicated a long life had been lived.

I gave him my respect, my time and silence, as he dropped his head to the side, laying it down on the soft grass, and then took his last breath.

The next morning, Adam was doing his rounds, and the old

geldings lifeless body caught his eye. He drove to the house to get Hazel and they both returned to pay their respects. Adam returned later to move the geldings body to a final resting place at the bottom of their farm.

The circle of life continued at the farm, with the welcome of new calves. Adam and Hazel had Black Angus cows and on our farm, there were brown and white Herefords. Sometimes the cattle would find their way on to the different properties, but it was always obvious when there was an odd one out. Bruce and Adam had a good friendship and shuffled the cattle back to their right sides of the fence when needed without fuss.

Most of the mares that visited my paddock were of a mature age, and most had been mothers before. There was a young mare on the farm with us, she was quite striking to look at, a coat of pitch black, with just a small white star. Her name was Keira.

Keira had not been a mother before, and Abby hesitated allowing her to be paddock served.

"I've got no idea what she will be like Shadow, but remember she is new at this, you need to go easy and look after her ok." Abby said to me.

Well, if only we knew! Keira was quite an energetic and enthusiastic young mare and I was soon wishing that she had not entered my paddock! She chased me around day and night. I could not get away from her. I'd go for a walk to the dam, and she would follow... so I would pick up a trot... and she would canter around in front of me and slide to a stop! Almost causing me to lose my balance and run straight into her.

Keira only stayed in the paddock with us a few weeks, Abby recognised that she was wearing me out, and decided to allow me a break.

Thankfully, my work paid off and Keira's enthusiasm produced an exquisite foal eleven months later.

"Are you seeing what I am seeing?" Abby said to Bruce as they stood near the small yards, watching the foal.

I was a Chestnut Tobiano, a pinto. Keira was pitch black. The foal was a rich mahogany bay, with four white stockings and a thick white blaze right down her face.

Bruce scratched his head, thinking.

"Who does she look like to you?" Abby said.

"Oh, oh wow. Ok, yes I see what you mean." Bruce replied, a tone of bewilderment in his voice.

Abby named the foal Pebbles, astounded by the colour and markings of the baby. I heard them laugh about the television show called The Flintstones, Fred and Barney, and Fred's daughter was called Pebbles.

But Pebbles was my foal wasn't she? Surely Fred didn't...

"I'm going to have to have to have a DNA comparison done Bruce, this is a little weird looking!" Abby laughed. "I can do a

DNA kit, and the Society can just do a parentage confirmation with the DNA of Shadows they already have on file."

Bruce laughed, it was obvious who he thought Pebbles father was. What did I think? Well any other mare I would have been sure, but the way Keira hassled me, well she could have hassled Fred easily enough too. He wouldn't have had to do much!

Considering Keira was so willing to become a mother, she did not adjust to having a foal well. She would not let Pebbles have anything to drink, I don't think she understood what she was trying to do.

Bruce wrapped some towel around a pipe, and Abby used it to accustom Keira to having her teats manipulated. It must be a strange thing to get used to, allowing a foal to feed from you, in an area that would not have been touched before.

Every time Pebbles tried to drink, Keira would squeal and kick up her leg. Bruce had to grab Pebbles out of the way to avoid her copping a kick from Keira.

So Abby got the towel covered pipe and spent hours rubbing Keira, desensitising her to having her teats touched. It paid off, and Keira accepted the process. By morning she was totally smitten with her new baby, and allowed her to feed without assistance or interference from Abby.

The next mare Abby brought to my paddock was the lovely Monalisa. Both Abby and Bruce were thrilled with our first baby Khaleesi and were keen to see if we could produce another just as nice. Monalisa stayed in my paddock for a couple of months and then moved out to the bigger paddock on the hill, with some of the other mares.

New life was again being created at our farm, in the form of human life as well. Abby's middle had grown, and it became obvious that there was a fourth little person on the way. It was again a happy time.

AMY CURRAN

CHAPTER TWENTY FIVE

By the start of Autumn all of the outside mares had returned to their homes, including the two stock horses that had come all the way from Western Australia. I had Scarlett for company and we were enjoying the peace of the quiet months. We only saw Monalisa and the other mares occasionally, if they came to the fence line to say hello. Usually they stayed around the lower gullies though, it was warmer and more sheltered in those parts.

Bruce did his usual rounds in his truck, checking the fences, dams, cattle and mares. One afternoon he seemed to take a lot longer than usual in the hill paddock. I tried to see where his truck had gone. I walked along the fence line until I caught glimpse of a shiny reflection. The sun hit the side mirror of his truck, and I could see he was stopped just at the bottom of one of the small hills.

I could not make out why he was stopped, I first thought maybe he was collecting firewood, but there were no fallen trees where he was parked, and the children weren't there to help him as they usually would.

My eye caught movement and I turned to see some of the mares walking around the dam, just below where Bruce was parked.

They had their heads down, but were not grazing. Were they sad? It was hard to tell from the distance.

One was missing. My heart sank.

Monalisa, where was she? My eyes darted to each of the mares, checking and double checking to see if I had missed her, if she was behind one of the others.

I looked back towards Bruce, making a path with my eyes from the mares to Bruce, and back again. No sight of Monalisa at all. I moved down the fence line and tried to see around the parked truck. And then, it caught my eye.

A body. A sleek beautiful body of bay, with black mane and tail.

Monalisa.

I would learn later that my dear Monalisa had been bitten by a snake, one of Australia's deadly Brown Snakes. She would not have suffered, it would more than likely not have been a prolonged passing.

Abby did not come straight away, it concerned me that I had not seen her at the farm, especially after the tragedy that took Monalisa. However, I understood her absence when she did come, holding her precious baby Charlotte in her arms.

Again, after death there was new life once more.

Charlotte was destined to be the most horsey child out of the lot. She was glued to Abby like a koala in a pouch. Everywhere

Abby went, Charlotte went too. They would come and say hello to Scarlett and I, and Charlotte would reach over the fence and grab our nostrils. It tickled, and made both of us snort.

I overheard Abby one afternoon tell Bruce that the DNA results for Pebbles had come back, and she was my foal. I don't think Bruce believed her, it really was a spitting image of Fred, but they say science doesn't lie.

Monalisa's foal was the only planned one for the season that was now upon us, so Abby and Bruce had a season without foals or weaning. I looked forward to seeing what outside mares may be arriving.

I didn't have to wait long, when a trailer arrived late one afternoon with two coloured mares aboard. Both part Arabian mares and both with striking pinto patterns.

One of them in particular caught my attention, Tipsy. A bright bay mare with stark white patches and a black mane and tail. She was ready to go the second she got off the trailer. Abby was holding my lead, but I let her know it was time.

"Are you serious Shadow? Right now? Hold her Stace!" Abby said to her friend who was holding Tipsy, "Shadow says its go time!"

And with the ok from Abby, I did my job. Love at first sight, it was meant to be.

Abby then moved us to the paddock, and Tipsy went off to explore the surrounds.

Just A Shadow

At the end of the season, the mare that came with Tipsy was picked up and taken back to her home. Tipsy stayed though, to have her foal at the farm with us. Abby liked Tipsy too.

Summer was fading to make way for the Autumn months and Bruce decided to take Scarlett and I up to Grandmas property, just ten minutes up the road. There were no other horses or cattle on Grandmas place and her paddocks were full of thick grass. Bruce said that she could do with some horses there to get the grass down, and thought that it was the perfect hideaway for Scarlett and I.

Grandma was a funny lady, she wasn't used to having horses around, but she adored us. Every day she would come out into the paddock and talk to us, and feed us treats. When I say treats, I mean human treats. Grandma didn't seem to know what horses ate, but we weren't going to tell her. I had my first taste of pink iced finger buns from Grandma, I had been missing out! They were outstanding! The sweet hit your taste bud's straight away, and the sticky icing would stick to the roof of our mouths, causing us to show our teeth and move our tongue in all directions in an attempt to loosen the bun.

The only other animals at Grandmas place was her dog Indy, and a bunch of chickens. The chickens shared our paddock and went between the fences into the house yard as well. They scurried and scratched under the pine trees every morning, looking for worms.

Grandmas house was right near a road, it was quite a busy road, and I wasn't used to the activity and noise of the cars. I liked to stand and watch the different vehicles as they drove past, there were a lot of trucks too.

Next door a lady taught horse riding, and the next house passed her a lady grew vegetables for the markets. It was an impressive looking vegetable patch! I wished I could get a closer look.

I decided that one day I would try and get a closer look at the vegetable patch. I waited until Grandma had left to go into town for the day and I started to play with the latch of the gate. It didn't take long, and the metal ring flicked off. The gate slowly swung open.

Scarlet raised her head to see what I was up to, and sniggered. I didn't expect her to follow, she was far too sensible.

Off I went, down alongside the road. Cars beeped their horns and I heard children laugh out of their windows as they saw me go past. What a sight I must've been, especially to those who weren't from the country. A brightly coloured horse wandering down the main road.

I arrived at the fence of the vegetable patch and tried to find a way in. Trucks roared past behind me, I had to be quick, some one was sure to stop and try and catch me soon.

Rows of green stems and lush covered vegetables. It was irresistible.

I jumped the fence, straight in I went! I trotted right into the middle of the patch and started to devour all that was before me. It was bliss! I had never tasted so many different types of vegetables and greens.

I'm not sure how long I had been amongst the vegetables, but it must have been some time as I was starting to feel an ache in my belly. A car pulled up, skidding to a stop, followed by another. A lady jumped out, and frantically started running towards me.

"Oh my god! My vegetables! Sid please, get him out!" The lady was not happy at all.

The man jumped in and grabbed me by my mane to stop me eating any more. "Well grab me a rope, quick!"

The lady came over with a rope, and screamed at me. "You bad horse! How dare you! I just got a big contract for these vegetables, they were going to be sold to restaurants! And look what you have done!"

No wonder they were so good I thought.

Another car pulled up and a lady jumped out with a halter and lead and ran over to me.

"It's ok, Ive called Abby, she knows he is out and I will take him back for her." The nice lady said. Her name was Elisa.

"Is she going to pay for my vegetables?!" The lady screamed.

Elisa ignored her and hurried me out of the vegetable patch and out onto the side of the road. "Wow you really got on her nerves didn't you, silly fella you."

I liked Elisa, she thought it was funny now that we were out of eye sight of the lady. She walked me back up through Grandmas gate and let me loose with Scarlet.

"Try and stay in here ok?" She laughed, as she closed and latched the gate behind her.

I saw the man from the vegetable patch come up later that afternoon and leave a note for Grandma in her letterbox. I guessed it was not a very nice note.

CHAPTER TWENTY SIX

Abby and the children visited Scarlett and I at Grandmas every few days, I loved watching the kids play in the yard while Abby checked on us, and gave us some food. The kids were hilarious chasing the chickens.

Most of Abby's time was spent looking after the children, but she loved taking photos. I'm blessed that she took so many photos of me, mostly in the paddock naturally, but one time she organised a session with Jolene.

Jolene wore an Indian headdress and outfit, and at dusk we walked out into the paddock. It was a magical time of day, the sun was streaming across the paddock, catching the long grass in its path, and backlighting Jolene and I.

They were amazing images, and I felt so special looking after Jolene while she sat on top of my back, on top of the world. Abby's friend Kym was there too and helped show me where to stand so Abby could take the photos from the right spot.

The photos that resulted that day would later be seen right around the world. Two of them in Abby's book 'Furfriends - a collective of children and their animal friends', which won medals in Moscow and Tokyo, and one of the photos would be awarded a Highly Commended award out of entries from all over the world in an exhibition in Las Vegas. My face was around the world.

Life continued at the farm while Scarlett and I were at Grandmas. Abby kept me informed, and told me that two foals had been born through the season. Kay had a strong chestnut colt, and sweet Tipsy had a filly that was a spitting image of me.

Kays competition name was 'Love is in the Air', so Abby called her colt 'Aliyah Comere Loverboy', which was apparently also a tribute to someone called Patrick Swayze that she would often talk about.

Tipsy's baby was 'Aliyah Tiana Belle' and she sounded absolutely divine.

Even though I had been retired from the show ring for some time now, I still attracted attention from the media. The Editor of the Australian Arabian Horse News called Abby and asked to do an article on me, where I was now, and what I was up to.

Abby was very excited, and took a photo of me running in the paddock with Scarlett especially for it. The article didn't talk much about my show results, more importantly what a gentle, reliable stallion I had become, and how I had proven myself as an ambassador for the temperament of Arabian horses.

Abby told the magazine that I was the only horse she trusted with her 'first ride' back after having a baby, that the bond she had with me was not like the other horses.

The article though, made Abby wonder if she was doing me justice, keeping me to herself in a paddock in the mountains, rather than allowing me the exposure I was worthy of, being out in the public eye, and being more accessible to mares who would possibly be bred to me if I was in a more central location.

Abby was also worried that I was bored in the paddock at grandmas, as they were spending a lot of time going away to dog shows. It was easier for them to show the dogs, rather than the other horses, and Bruce had said it was a lot less expensive as well. She felt guilty that I was stuck in the paddock all the time and didn't get to go anywhere. I wish I was able to tell her how content I was.

Abby and Bruce tried to find me a new home that would keep me busy, and they placed an advertisement in the horse deals magazine. I tried to tell Abby that I didn't need to be busy, I loved our life on the farm!

The calls came in, Abby seemed to be answering calls every time I saw her. I started to get worried. I just had to trust her that she would find me the right place, I knew she loved me and cared about me a lot, and that was why she was doing this. I wish I could have told her that I didn't want to go anywhere else.

"I just can't do it Bruce!" Abby said, yelling at Bruce as they walked around the corner of the shed.

"You can't just give him away Abby, that's stupid!" Bruce yelled back.

"I haven't liked the sound of anyone who has called about him, I just can't bear the thought of losing contact with him, and having on control over where he goes now or in the future. The man from overseas! No way! I could not do that to Shadow. And almost everyone that has called has been a male, Shadow is a ladies Stallion, he always has been."

Bruce raised his eyebrows.

"You know what I mean Bruce! He would not cope being owned solely by a male, or as a mans horse, without a lady. He is too kind and soft, you know that." Abby continued on. "Emma wanted to use him over some of their mares, and I think its a good solution. They can't afford to buy a Stallion like him, and we aren't using him, he is going to waste."

I tried to get Abby's attention, there was nothing wasting here, I loved it here! I wish she would let me stay.

"Righto, I still thinking 'giving him away' is stupid, we paid a lot of money for that horse." Bruce said begrudgingly.

"We are not giving him away, he is our horse and always will be. He will always be registered in our name, and I will do up a lease agreement."

"Yeah well, they'd want to look after him seeing they're getting out of paying for him, and paying any service fees!" Bruce said.

"I am sure they will," Abby replied, and they turned back to the house.

If only Abby knew what would happen next.

I had never seen Emma before, but I assumed it was her who had pulled up in the truck and trailer a few days later. Abby went to the front of the house to meet her, and then came to the paddock with two halters and leads.

"Scarlett will be no fuss to you, or any mares that you put in with Shadow" I could hear Abby talking.

"Oh, didn't I tell you?" Emma said, "we can't take the mare as well, we just can't have a horse there not doing anything if you know what I mean?"

Scarlett wasn't coming? My mouth gaped. Abby looked just as surprised, I could see her shoulders fall with disappointment.

"Oh, umm, ok, well I guess they will be ok," Abby said very unsure.

Emma was more forceful, and seemed to be trying to grab me before Abby could change her mind. I didn't want to make it any harder for Abby, so I did as I was told. I walked out of the paddock, and up into the trailer by the side of the road.

As the trailer pulled off, I couldn't even bear to look behind. I didn't want to see Abby's face, or Scarlett, I was so sad.

AMY CURRAN

CHAPTER TWENTY SEVEN

It was around an hours drive to Cedric Park. The truck turned onto the dirt driveway and all I could see were billows of dust pluming up the sides of the trailer. I could vaguely make out the shape of some small ponies on one side of the drive and as we neared the end of the straight drive, some houses.

The truck came to an abrupt stop, and I whacked my nose on the window. OUCH. I blinked my eyes, which were now watering from the impact. Through the dust I saw Emma go towards the house.

I waited for her to come back. It seemed like I was waiting for a long time, but eventually she did come back and lead me out into a large paddock.

There were no other horses in the paddock, it was very large, but there was not much to eat either. The ground was hard, and thick plant stalks were scattered throughout the dirt. I was not sure what they had been growing in the paddock before it was harvested, but the stalks were everywhere and they were painful to walk on.

I wandered around aimlessly for a little while, before choosing a spot along one of the fences to rest for the night.

Dogs woke me the next morning, running past the fences, barking at each other as they went. I watched them run off into the distance and could just make out the outline of a group of horses on one of the far hills.

The day progressed and the hot sun beat down upon my back. Even though only an hour away from home, it seemed much hotter here. I wandered around trying to find a tree or shade to escape the heat, but there was none. No trees! I'd never been in a paddock without any trees or shelter before, never even seen one. Even at Chellville and where I was born, where the paddocks were smaller, there were shelters to escape the heat. Not here.

I couldn't see a lot from my paddock, but I could hear the sounds of other horses, trucks and trailers. I thought there were a lot of other horses, going by the noises, I just couldn't see them. I was so lonely.

Emma had a husband called Jack. He did most of the work on Cedric Park, he was always going up and down the driveways, dogs chasing behind. He would occasionally stop to check my water trough while on his quad bike, but he never stayed long. He was always gone again by the time I got up there. I craved contact, I wasn't used to being so ignored. I guess they had a lot of horses to tend to.

It wasn't long before I would have contact again though, as Jack and Emma had jobs for me to do.

"Gotta get our monies worth outta the old fella" I heard Jack say as he led a mare towards my gate.

"What money?" Emma laughed, "deal of the century this! Free foals!"

Jack laughed with her. It was already obvious that I was seen as a commodity here.

I welcomed the mare though, and enjoyed the company. She stayed with me for a couple of months and a few other mares did the same, coming and going after I had done my job. There was no excitement or praise here, like with Abby, there was an expectation of me that I had to earn my place and I would just do my job.

As the last mare of the season was taken out of my paddock, I accepted loneliness once more. The general background noise around Cedric Park had lessened, as the other stallions had also finished their seasons. I couldn't see the other stallions close up, but I could smell there were several of them and hear their calls as they tried to get the attention of the mares.

I would later learn there were over sixty horses on Cedric Park, and all were there for a purpose. There wasn't any personal attention, the horses were just treated like a part of the job, I don't think I saw a single pat handed out the whole time I was there.

The months rolled on slowly, and I got more and more depressed. There was nothing to eat on the ground, and the water in the trough was thick and muddy. Without grass to cover the dirt, the dust billowed around my face all day, stinging my eyes.

Jack and Emma drove up to the gate of the paddock one morning, and got out to check the water level in the trough.

"Pretty gross Jack," Emma said.

"Yeah well, not much we can do about it, its a bloody waste of a paddock having him in here you know?' Jack said.

"Yes, shove him out the back, he is looking awful, don't want anyone to see him."

Jack moved me out to the back of the property, into a paddock that had lots of young Thoroughbreds in it. As we walked towards the paddock I perked up a little, excited at the idea of company.

How wrong I was.

CHAPTER TWENTY EIGHT

We got to the gate, and Jack hurriedly led me through, took off the halter, and quickly ducked back out of the gate again. I stood, looking around, and could see at least 15 other horses, all of them much bigger, much younger, and a lot fitter than me. They were Thoroughbreds, the breed used for racing. They were like a mob of young thugs and I was just an old man who wanted to live peacefully.

I had become weak from the lack of feed in the other paddock and my weeping eyes, caused by the dust, had started to become infected. I felt miserable on the inside and am sure I looked just as miserable on the outside as well.

The 'alpha horse' in the paddock was a tall bay colt, with long thick legs, and a sleek torso. He was built for racing, that was obvious. He pranced up to me, tossing his head as he came closer. As he reached my side, I noticed how big he really was. He towered over me, must have been close to 17hh, a giant next to me at 15hh.

He came right up along side me and pushed his nose into my neck, snuffling and snorting, asserting his dominance. I closed my eyes, I just wanted him to leave me alone.

The big colt seemed to be frustrated by my lack of fight, and reached out and bit the crest of my neck.

Ouch!

He reared, signaling me to fight back. I did not. I was weak. Reduced to a walking skeleton almost, and now the last ounce of pride I had was being sucked from me by a horse a quarter of my age. I lowered my head in submission, and he leaped up into a canter, and went back to the rest of the herd. I wandered slowly down along the fence line, looking for a corner to rest, away from any further confrontation.

Every day a new colt would challenge me, asserting themselves, proving their stance in the pack to the others. I never fought back, some would say I was a coward. Why wouldn't I, the mighty stallion, show them my power and life skills... I didn't have it in me.

The colts would take turns biting my skin, ripping the hair from me. I had little fat cover, the shape of my ribs and hips was now clearly visible through my hair. There was nothing to soften the pain of the bites and kicks, they all went straight to my bones, to my nerves. I'd never felt such excruciating pain and torture.

When they got sick of biting me, some would chew on my tail, my long glorious tail, until there were only mere strands left.

Jack and Emma would take turns driving to check the level of the water in the trough every few days, but would not stop to inspect me. I was 'out of sight, out of mind' for them.

There was even less grass here than the previous paddock, and to make it even worse there was competition for every blade of grass.

Occasionally a bale of hay would come over the fence, but by the time I could manage to get close enough, there was barely a few stalks left. I was starving, the emptiness inside me was unbearable.

As the weeks progressed I found it easier to lay down, rather than stand. My legs were tired, they could not hold me up, ironic considering I would have weighed the least I had ever weighed before.

The more I lay down, the harder it became to get up. That was ok, I didn't want to get up. I got thirsty, but I managed. I learnt to get up only during the night, when the air was cooler, and it didn't exhaust me as much. Also, at night the other horses would generally be asleep and would not notice my movement. I could avoid their cruel games.

Do you know what else was missing at night?

The reflection in the water, my reflection. I caught a glimpse of myself one day a few weeks ago, I was a sorry sight. Nothing but a mere shadow of my former self. As well as the obvious condition I was in, my dull coat made me look a completely different colour, I couldn't bear to look again.

My eyes had gotten so bad I couldn't open them all the way, the infected discharge had dried around my eye lids, making them feel like they were partly glued shut. It was a horrible feeling.

Just A Shadow

Days blurred into nights, and nights became days again. I barely noticed, but for a small slit of sunlight through what I could see out of my eyelids.

I believed my life was over, I was at the mercy of Jack and Emma and this horrible place.

CHAPTER TWENTY NINE

Early one morning there was a commotion, I heard the young colts race to the gate. I didn't bother lifting my head, I wouldn't have been able to see even if I had managed to turn my head the full way.

Next I heard footsteps, and a halter was put around my face.

"Get up! Come on, get up!" It was Jack. I couldn't move, he kicked me in the side. "Get up ya old bastard, bloody hell. Gotta get you outta here before ya die on us, that wont be good for us."

I was not sure where he was trying to take me, but anywhere had to be better than where i was in this moment. I pulled myself up, trying to block out the pain, and blindly followed out through the gate, and onto the horse trailer. I heard the tailgate shut, and I collapsed in a heap. I fell right to the floor of the trailer, and closed my eyes.

I awoke to the stop of the trailer and the sound of the truck door opening and closing. I was not sure how long we had been travelling for, but i knew I hadn't moved. I slowly opened my eyes, as much as I could. My rope wasn't tied up, just dangling where I was led on, not that I had the energy to make a great escape, they knew that. I lay quietly, waiting to hear the lowering of the tailgate.

"Hey Jack, how ya going?"

Who was that. That voice.

Jack was talking now, I was waiting to hear that voice again, I knew it... I knew I knew it!

"Is he in there? You sure you brought him back for me? Why can't I see him"?

My heart stopped.

"Oh he is in there, lazy bastards been having a nap, watch out, I'll open the ramp for you." Jack said.

The ramp dropped to the ground with a thud, and I waited to hear the voice again. Silence. Had they gone?

"I didn't bother tying him up, he's so quiet ya know! So just go on and in grab him, lazy bugger he is." Jacks voice pierced the silence.

I waited to hear the other voice.

Instead.... I felt a hand.

A soft hand ran along my flank, over my ribs. I felt the brush of jeans as the person gently slid across my legs, the hand on my shoulder now.

I heard no words, but in that moment I knew. I knew that I was safe.

Abby. I almost stopped breathing.

I think she had too at one point. I felt her long hair brush over my neck, and her arms go over my shoulder and my nose. She pressed her face into my neck as hard as she could.

"Oh Shadow." Was all she said as I felt her tremble.

It was love that got me on my feet, that was all it was. I had to get out of that trailer so I could stay with Abby, that was all I could think about.

Once out, Jack didn't waste any more time, and quickly lifted the ramp and drove out, obviously eager to escape any confrontation that may have been coming. Abby led me into the paddock, and took off my halter.

My legs became weak just from the short walk into the paddock, and I started to lay down. Abby put her hand on my shoulder, to try and support me as I went. As I sank into the grass, Abby collapsed beside me. I could barely see her, but I knew she was crying.

We stayed like that, together on the ground, for a long time. And I cherished every second of it. I was home and I had love.

I closed my eyes.

CHAPTER THIRTY

When I awoke, I noticed Abby had gone and come back again. She had brought some hay with her, and a soft cotton rug. And small people! There were small people, Bruce and Abby's small people, MY small people!

I lifted myself up onto my legs, and they each came towards me with an armful of things. Charli and James put down some of the hay on the ground in front of me, Hannah had a brush, and Jolene was carrying the cotton rug. Abby closed the gate behind them, and came over too.

"Just put it down there kids, he will eat it." Abby said.

"He needs way more than this mummy, why didn't we bring more food for him? Charli asked.

"He will have more, but he is a bit sick, if he eats too much too quick he could get a big bad tummy ache. So we just have to give him lots of little meals all throughout the day, little bits at a time." Abby explained.

I could tell the small people were happy to see me, but they were staring at me strangely, looking at the outline of my bones. It made them sad.

Hannah brushed some of the loose hair from my dull coat, and Jolene slid the rug over onto my back. Abby helped them do up the buckles, and they watched me eat the rest of the hay.

"Come on kids, lets give him some time now to rest, he needs to rest to get some strength back too." Abby said, and they headed back to the gate.

I was full of love, food, and cloaked in a warm soft rug.

I did not sleep well this first night, my legs were aching from the trip back, my hind legs went through phases of a pins and needles type feeling. I lay down, and it eased. I had become used to light sleep too, always needing to keep an eye on my surroundings.

Part way through the night I heard a familiar sound, the low hum of a diesel engine… Bruce? It was Bruce I knew it. I staggered to my feet and shuffled to where I could make out the headlights at the fence line.

I saw an outline of a man as I approached, broad shoulders, it certainly was Bruce. He walked towards me, put his hand on my neck and let out a sigh.

"Oh mate." he said. "I can't believe its you."

The tone of his voice was shaky, but Bruce wasn't one to be seen to cry in the time I had known him. He was a hard man on the outside, but in this moment, he too was broken. He ran his hand up and down my neck, and I nuzzled into his flannelette jacket.

He walked back to the truck, and returned with a small bucket of mash. He stood beside me, scooping up the mash in his hands, and hand feeding it to me.

"Just this much for now mate, Abby said we can't have you getting a belly ache straight up, be back to give you more tomorrow I promise."

Abby returned at first light, with some lucerne hay, and a small bucket. She held the bucket for me, and I nibbled up the mash with as much appreciation as I could muster.

"Its ok buddy, we know you love it, just take it easy ok, baby steps." Abby said softly.

The mash stuck to my gums, and I lifted my mouth out of the bucket and curled my lip. Abby laughed. I needed her laugh, every time I heard Abby laugh my fire inside grew stronger.

Bruce and Abby came with buckets of mash several times each day, as well as some hay to keep me going in between. The paddock had quite nice feed, not too rich that I may scour, but enough that I had plenty to eat, the dirt was covered and there was no dust.

There was a young girl who checked my water every second day, I loved having the people activity around me again.

One evening, Abby brought down a heavy doona rug, to give me some extra warmth. She draped it over my back, and went around the front to do up the buckles. I tried to stand, I really did, it was such a comfy rug. It was just too heavy for me. I laid down.

"Oh Shadow, what's wrong buddy," Abby was concerned.

I came to a rest on the ground, and put my neck down flat on the ground.

"The rug? Don't tell me the rug is too heavy? Oh wow, oh Shadow."

Abby pulled off the rug, and rubbed my neck. I stood up and nuzzled into her chest.

"Your legs are swollen too mate, just rest up ok, take it easy, you don't need to do anything now. I am going to go and see a friend who owns a saddlery, we will just have to build up your rugs gradually ok? You'll be ok I promise. The vet is going to come and check on you tomorrow too."

I hated the idea of the vet, but when the vehicle pulled up, and I saw she was a lady vet, I was pleasantly surprised. This wouldn't be so bad after all I thought.

"Hey big boy, how are you feeling," the vet said. She had a nice voice, and small hands.

"This is Tammy, Shadow," Abby said, "you let her look at you now ok."

I nuzzled the vet's chest, and she laughed, "He is a smooch isn't he!"

"Oh gosh is he ever haha, our nickname for him has always been Mr Clooney, you can see why!" Abby replied.

Vet Tammy checked my gut sounds, and my heart. She moved along to my face and took a good look at my eyes.

"They are definitely infected, poor boy. Its hard to tell if there is anything foreign inside irritating them, but it does look like a prolonged infection, possibly caused by dust or dirt. Come past the clinic when we are done here and I will give you some cream to apply every day. Just give them a good wash with some warm salty water first, like you've been doing, then the cream."

I liked the warm water on my face, it was so relaxing. When Abby would finish with my face, she always dried it with a towel too, and as she rubbed up and down, I would push into the towel, tricking her into giving me a head scratch at the same time.

Vet Tammy walked back to her vehicle, and came back with a bucket of bits and pieces. All I could see was a bottle and some gloves. Sure, there were other interesting things in there too, but Abby held my lead, so I couldn't get close enough.

The gloves came out, and Tammy started to put them on. Wow! They were huge gloves, they went right up to her armpits. I wondered why she was putting them on for, was she going to do some gardening? Washing up?

She finished putting them on, and walked around behind me, where I couldn't see her. I felt her lift up my tail, and wondered what she was.... Yikes!

That was the single most strangest sensation I had felt in my life. I was just about paralysed, not game to move. Charlotte (smallest person) was watching as well, and had a look on her face I had not seen before. Her eyes were big, and she was not saying a word.

"Ill take this back to the clinic and have a stool sample done, see if we can get a worm count." Vet Tammy yelled to Abby as she removed her gloved hand and walked back around to the front of me. She made a knot in the glove, which now looked like a plastic bag full of poop.

CHAPTER THIRTY ONE

By my second week home, I was able to wear a winter weight rug. It was only a 600g fill, but it was certainly better than feeling the raw chill of the wind on my bones. Abby checked it every night to make sure it hadn't slipped during the day, or started to rub me.

The small people liked to help check my rugs as well, and they were becoming little experts at my daily routine. I didn't mind what they did, as long as they visited me. I loved to listen to them play. While I was eating dinner they would run around and around the paddock, chasing each other and giggling at the top of their lungs. Home was such a happy place.

"You've got a spark in your eye again my mate," Abby said one morning. I certainly was starting to feel better, each day I was another day further away from the pain.

Abby was also doing as the Vet ordered, and treating my eyes with the cream every day. It was so cold as it came out of the tube and into my eyes, but I could already tell that it was making a difference. I could open my eyes easily, and my face wasn't getting as dirty from the infection that had been draining.

"A few more days and I reckon your eyes will be good as new Shadow," Abby had said one morning after putting the cream in. "And, on the weekend I have a special treat for you coming too! One of my oldest friends Ginny is coming to see you, and have a bit of a feel of your muscles, see if you might be sore anywhere.

That sounded nice. Soon enough it was the weekend and Ginny pulled up in her car. Abby went out to meet her, and together they came into the paddock.

"You are magnificent aren't you Shadow," Ginny said. I liked her already.

Abby took my rugs off and gave my coat a brush. Ginny ran her hands over my back and hindquarters.

"I won't be able to do any muscle work for him today Abby," Ginny said sadly, "He has hardly any muscle cover there, the poor boy. Let's do some red light therapy for him."

I wasn't sure what this red light therapy was, so I watched Ginny intently as she went to her bag, and pulled out two black rods. She turned them on, and the ends lit up with a red light.

"See these Shadow? These little red lights will hopefully ease some of your pain, it wont hurt. I'm just going to run them along some of your muscles and your acupoints." Ginny explained.

Abby was listening too, and watching as Ginny held the lights on two different parts of my body, her arms apart.

"Oh Shadow!" Abby laughed as I let out a big yawn.

"That's good!" Ginny exclaimed! "Yawning is great, it means he is responding to the treatment, lets see if he yawns again."

Ginny moved the lights around to another muscle, and sure enough, I yawned again. It was an incredible feeling, my muscles were unwinding and a rush of relaxation was sweeping through me.

"The record is 17!" Ginny laughed, as I yawned again.

Abby was laughing as well, "he really is enjoying it isn't he."

Ginny moved down my hind legs, and explained to Abby that there was an acupoint there that was linked to my eyes. If she could penetrate the point, it may help ease my eye irritations. Abby watched my eyes as Ginny held the light onto the inside of my hock.

Amazingly, my eyes started to weep, as if relaxing also.

"Oh wow," Abby said to Ginny, "that's amazing!"

"He has responded beautifully, I am very happy with him, he is a lovely boy. We might stop it there though for this session, we don't want to over do it on him. I would love to come back and do another session on him in a few weeks." Ginny said.

"We would absolutely love you to" Abby replied.

Abby put my rugs back on, and removed my halter and lead. I

was asleep before they got in the car.

The next day I could feel a suppleness in my muscles that had not been there the day before. I walked around the paddock, enjoying the crisp morning air, and feeling the breeze flow through my forelock. I was by the water trough when I heard Abby over near my feed bin, and I turned to walk towards her. I picked up a brisk walk.

"Look at you go Shadow!" Abby said, "a spring in your step today boy hey?"

I jumped up into a trot, and 1, 2, 3, 4 did four big steps for her. She ran to me, arms outstretched and wrapped herself around my neck.

"You did a trot Shadow! You did it!" She said through joyed tears.

It was the first time I had trotted in over a year. Just four steps, but a trot.

Just A Shadow

CHAPTER THIRTY TWO

I had so much to live for now that I was back home with Bruce and Abby and their children. Even though the weather was getting colder, the children still played around my paddocks, just on odd afternoons. James would push his dump truck up and down the fence line, while Charlotte showed me her toy horses through the fence. I would blow air on them with my nose, and she would giggle.

Jolene and Hannah helped Abby brush me, and check my rugs. I liked to play games with them if they were carrying the bucket, it always made them laugh. They would try and get over the fence, and make it to my feed bin before I could reach them with the bucket. They'd climb over and make a beeline for the feed bin, while I would try and shove my head in the bucket while they were still holding it. Their hands would swap the bucket side to side, trying to dodge my head, ducking and weaving all the way to the feed bin, where they would pour it in as quick as they could. Then, they'd let out a big laugh as I dove my head into the feed, like I had not seen it for a month.

I loved spending time with them, they never asked me to do anything, and every single one of them wanted me to get better.

I could wear three rugs now, a nice soft cotton one on the bottom, then a thick warm doona, topped with a waterproof rug that kept the wind out.

It was lucky that I could wear three rugs too, we couldn't have timed that better. This particular night was freezing, but it was a different type of cold. There was a cold chill in the air, however an absence of strong wind or rain. I huddled down in the corner of the paddock, and settled in for the night.

The next morning, I awoke to the strangest thing I had ever seen. The ground was white! The trees were white! Everything was white! My eyes took a while to adjust to the bright glare of my surrounds.

"Snow! Shadow, snow!" Abby yelled as she jumped the fence. "Come on, quick quick, its freeeeezing and I have your warm mash!"

I lifted my legs to walk... but my hooves felt so heavy. They were packed full with the stuff that Abby was calling snow. I felt like I was wearing super high platform shoes! I had to lift my legs so high, up from the knees! I could hear Abby laughing.

"Oh Shadow, are you actually ok? Is it just the snow, is that why you're walking like that?" Abby said as I got closer.

I stopped near the bucket of warm mash, and as I ate Abby inspected my feet. She got all of the packed in snow out, and I was level with the ground again. She gave me a hug.

"That was kind of funny mate," and she kissed my face.

Although it was pretty, I was thankful that the snow did not last more than a day. By the afternoon most of it had melted and given way to the grass beneath, and the frozen sheet of ice on the top of my water had also disappeared.

By the next morning, only a few patches of white remained, around the edges of the paddock where the sun did not reach as much.

Abby told me that the next day a nice man was coming to make my hooves feel nice again. She said he was a 'Master Farrier', and explained that meant that he would be able to have me all balanced and comfortable again.

"He is not going to put any metal shoes on you Shadow, he will just look at your hooves and shape them back to how they are supposed to be. You be brave ok." I pushed her lovingly. Abby was trying so hard to make me feel better. I think she was beating herself up a lot about letting me go to that place. Oh Abby. She wasn't to know.

The next morning the farrier arrived, his name was Mark. He got out of his truck and started to carry some tools down to my fence. I hadn't had my hooves looked at for so long, I was worried this was going to hurt.

Out of the passenger side of his truck, came his wife. She had big thick curly hair, and a smile just as big. Her name was Annie.

"Hello big boy!" she beamed "My, you are a gorgeous boy in the flesh aren't you, I have heard so much about you." I liked her straight away.

Mark had grabbed the tools he needed, a long bumpy rasp, a hoof stand, and some smaller nippers and cutters. He didn't say a lot, I think it was Annie's job to say things, she said a lot, and she laughed a lot like Abby does.

"Come on Annie pay attention, put on his halter, we don't know this horse and he is a Stallion remember." Mark said.

Annie got the halter and lead and put it around my head. "I really don't think he is going anywhere" she said to Mark.

"Just hold him will you." Mark replied, rolling his eyes at her.

Mark was so gentle, he only needed to use the cutters a little, he spent most of the time gently rasping, checking the shape of my hooves, and rasping again. He was very particular and was definitely an expert. It was hard to hold up my legs for long, so Mark let me have breaks in between, where I could stand on four legs.

It was very cold, because of the snow the day before I think. Annie was cold as well, and she was snuggled right into my chest. I had three rugs on, including a big black quilted Doona rug, and I pushed forward into Annie, inviting her to get closer and warmer. She accepted, and gently slid her arms along my shoulders and into the warmth of my rugs. Like a big bear hug. She rested her head on my neck and we both closed our eyes.

Before I knew it, Mark was finished. I think Annie and I must have both fallen asleep briefly!

"Annie! Come on, we are done, get out of there." Mark said. He was trying to be stern, but Annie knew he didn't mean it.

"Isn't he lovely!" She said to him.

Mark just laughed. "Come on, I have to get you to your shop."

I felt so much better with my feet done, Mark had filed down my heels, and I could walk evenly again. Over the following days the swelling in my legs started to go down as well, I could feel every ounce of the circulation returning.

Being able to move around nice again was wonderful, I finally got to explore the paddock that I had arrived into, which was alongside a nursing home. Abby had chosen this paddock for me, as she was worried that being with my old friends would be too much to start with, she said I had to get better first.

Along the front of the paddock was a walk way, a concrete path that lots of people used for jogging and walking their dogs. It was quite a busy pathway, and now that I could walk around I enjoyed following alongside people as they went by. Some of them brought me carrots, Abby really needed to make a sign to tell them that I preferred apples, but I took bites out of the carrots that were offered to me to be polite.

The folks that lived in the nursing home would come out and say hello to me as well. Some of them could walk by themselves, some of them had metal frames to help them, and occasionally one would come out in a wheel chair. They always had nurses to help them, and the nurses liked me as well. If it was my only job now to make people happy, then I was going to do that as best I could.

One Sunday afternoon Abby arrived with my dinner, and another car pulled up behind. A young boy and his parents got out, and walked down towards me. My small people knew him and yelled out to him to follow them.

"Curtis, come on buddy! Come and play with us!" He smiled and ran down to the fence. Abby lifted him over and off they went, running through my paddock.

Abby came and took my rugs off and started to brush my coat.

"Wow he is looking heaps better," Curtis mum Jodie said. "He has definitely put on weight since those photos you showed me."

Abby and Jodie talked about me while I watched Curtis play with the other kids. They were having a great time, I loved having them around me.

Abby put my rugs back on, and gave me my dinner. The kids came running back over and Curtis gave me a big hug. I liked him a lot. Charli wanted to show him how she rode me, and Abby lifted her up on to my back. I could barely feel it when she was up there, I only knew she was there because she was a fidget. She never wanted to actually go for a ride, walk anywhere. She just sat up there for a few moments, on top of the world, and then asked Abby to lift her down.

Abby came to deliver my feed one afternoon, and I wasn't feeling the best. It was cold, and windy, but I was hungry. She called, and called "Come on Shadow, you've got to move my friend!"

I tried, but all I could manage was a faster walk. I just couldn't seem to find the step to jump into a trot.

"You're going to make me come and get you, aren't you?" she laughed. Oh how I loved that laugh. And then, Abby put down the bucket and ran over to me, my ears pricked with excitement! She was so much fun.

Abby got to me and gave me a big bear hug, and whispered "Come on Shadow, you can do it... I'll race ya!"

Well I couldn't knock back a race! As Abby turned and ran back to the feed bin, I leaped into a trot and ran straight along beside her. My muscles were loose, the chill in the air was filled with excitement, and we trotted right alongside each other, as if we were one.

We got to the feedbag and I slid to a stop beside Abby. She gave me another huge hug, as she said "I love you Shadow. I'm not letting you give up."

I was in heaven.

CHAPTER THIRTY THREE

As I was feeling a lot better, Abby decided to start taking me out for walks. Like a big dog, she would click a lead on my head stall, and off we would go outside the paddock. The kids came too, they thought it was a lot of fun to 'walk the big dog'. Passers by found it amusing as well, and lots of cars would slow down to get a better look at us.

The gate out of my paddock was behind the nursing home, so we would have to walk through the car park, and out of the driveway. Abby joked that it was because I was old now, I lived there. I didn't mind, if this was life being old I liked it!

Once out of the driveway we would follow the path along the side of the road and stop where there were green patches of grass. Abby would let me eat, while the kids chased each other up and down the path.

I enjoyed my visitors, especially the ones that brought apples. A lady called Helen came to visit me several times, and she always brought pink lady apples. She told me about a horse she had, her best friend, it made her cry to talk about him.

The bills to help me recover were mounting up, and Abby was

struggling to work out where she was going to find the extra money that was needed. As well as paying the vet, buying feed and paying for the separate paddock, she wanted to ensure that she was able to care for me for the rest of my life.

"I have an idea Shadow," she said to me one sunny morning as she took off my heavy rug. "You have had such an incredible life, you have been through so much more than most, I want to write a book about it."

A book? About me?

"Your life is pretty amazing when you think about it! A young foal, not even weaned, with a spinal injury. Your future wasn't looking so good at that stage was it?"

I did have to agree there.

"You recovered with the love from your master's wife, but then your first home away from your birth farm set you back as well. A stallion that rears and injures his Master, I think that was your second life right there."

Sarge, I still felt horrible about that day.

"You could have ended up anywhere after that, but luckily Betty and Craig came along. To go from that to Top Ten Australian National Champion Part Arabian Stallion? That's pretty impressive my boy. I see your third life flash just after this though, when you were reduced to the ground in re-training. If you weren't owned by Betty here your life could have been over."

Abby was right, putting it all out in a summary like this, I could see how lucky I was, how I met pathways where my life could have gone in either direction.

"Your fourth life? A stallion that had a horrible reputation as being dangerous, and having 'wobbles' being advertised for sale. I don't even want to think about where you could have ended up, but Betty saved you here by choosing Trudy. She loved you very much as well. You'd certainly established yourself as a ladie's stallion at this point!"

I smirked, Abby loved to call me Mr Clooney, the ladies man.

"Fork in the road number five buddy, when Trudy was forced to sadly find you a home. She had the offer from the man overseas, but lucky for you she declined it. And you met us!" Abby gave a big laugh.

I pushed her with my head, I liked this part of the story!

"Life number six... I am sorry Shadow, I can't talk about it. It is still too close for me. Know I am sorry please, I should never have let you go. I thought that leasing you would have ensured that you were safe, I couldn't bear to sell you, not knowing where you would end up, but look what happened instead. I really thought I was doing the best thing for you."

Poor Abby, she really needed to stop beating herself up.

"I promise you will die with me. I just hope that's a long way down the track yet."

CHAPTER THIRTY FOUR

Abby enjoyed writing my book, and kept me updated on how she was progressing. She was talking on the phone to Betty a lot, it was so special that they had each other. Betty was happy to know where I was and that I was safe, and Abby was fascinated learning all about my past.

Abby started to promote the book on the internet, building up interest, and sourcing information. A lady contacted her one day, with a simple message that read

Are you the person who was breeding the 'Aliyah' horses?

Abby responded straight away and asked if she had one, to which she replied she did! The lady's name was Briana, and the horse she had was Aliyah Tiana Belle. My daughter with Tipsy. Memories came flooding back.

As a foal, Tiana Belle was sold to a family in Sydney, who had promised to show her, and keep in touch with Abby. Sadly, they did not, and had not registered their details as new owners with any of the societies.

Briana had seen Tiana Belle advertised a few years later, and bought her straight away. She loved her markings, and could see she was a well bred filly. Unfortunately, when she arrived, Tiana Bella was in very poor condition. She was underweight and covered from head to tail in rain scald, her coat scabbed and red.

Briana spent a lot of time getting her better, and noticed she also had an eye injury that had been untreated. They competed together at the Pinto Nationals and won Champion 2-3 year old Filly!

In a horrible twist of fate though, Tiana Belles eye then became worse, and she needed to have surgery. Her short, but very impressive, show career was over.

Abby straight away offered to bring Tiana Belle home, but it seemed she had the same luck with second chances as I did. Her new owner Briana adored her, and promised to stay in touch and give her an easy life.

You've got to wonder where these second chances come from, but I am so thankful.

Though Abby's research, and those she was in contact with already, it is known where most of my progeny are, and they are dearly loved, in all of the parts of Australia that they are. Two sisters are even together in Western Australia, Monalisa's daughter Khaleesi, and Willow, sisters only a year apart in age. Pebbles is still with Abby and Bruce, living with Malii amongst the mountains. My dear Kay is with us as well.

Looking back my life was full, I had experienced more than most could only dream of. I'd been lower than most, literally on deaths door, but at other times been on top of the world, and images of me seen around the world.

I have now been back home with Abby and her family for almost a year. My strength has returned and I am back living alongside my soul mate and true love, Scarlett.

Abby has promised that I will die with them, and so I have nothing to fear. My worries are over, and so my story ends. At twenty two years old, even if I died tomorrow, I would be content. I have nothing to prove, nothing left to achieve.

I am home.

THE END

AMY CURRAN

ABOUT THE AUTHOR

Amy Curran lives in the picturesque area of the Blue Mountains, in New South Wales, Australia. She is married to Scott, and together they enjoy spending time with their four children.

Amy finds inspiration in their animals which include Australian Cattle Dogs, Horses, Cattle and Ragdoll Cats.

Amy is the Author and Illustrator of several of the Early Readers in the series 'Tales of Tails' by Pink Coffee Publishing. 'Just A Shadow' is her first novel.

*Shadow at the
Australian National Arabian Championships*

Shadows grandfather 'Amir El Shaklan'

Shadows father 'Amirs Sandman' the Lotto Horse

Shadow and 'Trudy' overlooking the beach

Shadow on Show

'Orr Brae Sacred Summer'

Shadow and 'Craig'

The day Shadow and 'Bruce' met.

The connection was instant.

Shadow and 'Bruce' in the paddock, after he arrived home.

Scarlett following behind.

Shadow and 'Abby'

Just A Shadow

Shadow loves the freedom of his large paddocks

'Abby's first ride after having children and two years, Shadow was the horse she trusted the most. Shadow had also not been ridden for these years.

'Desert Fox Scarlett Lady'

Scarlett

'Monaliisa'ar'

'Heste Arabique Southern Belle'

Tipsy

Just A Shadow

*Shadow and Kay
Always the gentleman*

*Monalisa's foal
'Aliyah Khaleesi'
four days old
with Hannah*

*Tipsys foal
'Aliyah Tiana
Belle'
just two days old*

*Kays foal
'Gleniph
Kiss Me Kate'
aka Smooch*

Just A Shadow

Kays second foal with Shadow 'Aliyah Comere Loverboy'

Shadow and Jolene in 'Furfriends'

Shadows article in The Versatile Arabian Horse

Shadow the day he arrived back home

One month back

Just A Shadow

*Shadows
very enthusiastic
head rub!*

Happy to be home

Home for life

AMY CURRAN

ACKNOWLEDGEMENTS

The Author would like to acknowledge those who gave Shadow a future in his early days, taught him life skills, followed or played a part in his journey, or were simply there for him when he needed it most.

With special mention to
My husband Scott and children Jolene, Hannah, James and Charlotte

The late Lester Williams
Billie and Kurt Lewis
Tracey Turner
Allyson and John Sales
Sharon Meyers
Neil and Gillian Shepherd
Suzie Chalmers and Alexis
Joanne, Richard and Craig Dorin
Karen Bailey
Helen Rixon (the Apple lady)
Tiffany Fitzpatrick
Marian Duncan (who painted an exquisite portrait of Shadow that we treasure more than gold)
Anna and Mark Shaw
Dionne Arnold
Michelle Thomas
Joy Parker
Natalie & Oliver Silver
Dana Jenkerson
Sharni Radford
and all of those who pre-ordered this book.

www.ingramcontent.com/pod-product-compliance
Lightning Source LLC
Chambersburg PA
CBHW051946290426
44110CB00015B/2128